THE WORDS

931 - 8250

1700 St Antoine West

Guy, Lucien Alb

1001

Maisonneuve East

873 - 4444

8:30 → 4:30

JEAN-PAUL SARTRE

THE WORDS

TRANSLATED FROM THE FRENCH

BY BERNARD FRECHTMAN

VINTAGE BOOKS

A DIVISION OF RANDOM HOUSE · NEW YORK

First Vintage Books Edition, April 1981
Copyright © 1964 by George Braziller, Inc.
All rights reserved under International and Pan-American Copyright Conventions. Published in the United States by Random House, Inc., New York, and simultaneously in Canada by Random House of Canada Limited, Toronto. Originally published by George Braziller, Inc., New York, in 1964. Originally published in French under the title *Les Mots*. Copyright © 1964 by Librairie Gallimard

Library of Congress Cataloging in Publication Data
Sartre, Jean-Paul, 1905-
The words.
Translation of Les mots.
Reprint of the ed. published by G. Braziller, New York.
1. Sartre, Jean-Paul, 1905-   —Biography.
2. Authors, French—20th century—Biography. I. Title.
[PQ2637.A82Z513 1981]   848'.91409 [B]   80-6136
ISBN 0-394-74709-7

Manufactured in the United States of America

To Madame Z

Part 1 READING

Around 1850, in Alsace, a schoolteacher with more children than he could afford was willing to become a grocer. This unfrocked clerk wanted compensation. Since he was giving up the schooling of minds, one of his sons would school souls. There would be a minister in the family; it would be Charles. Charles stole away; he preferred to take to the road in quest of a circus rider. His portrait was turned to the wall, and the family was forbidden to mention his name. Whose turn was it? Auguste hastened to imitate the paternal sacrifice. He went into business and did well for himself. There remained Louis, who had no particular bent. The father took this quiet boy in hand and in less than no time made a minister of him. Later, Louis carried obedience to the point of likewise begetting a minister, Albert Schweitzer, whose career is public knowledge. Meanwhile, Charles had not found his circus rider. His father's noble gesture had left its mark on him: all his life he retained a passion for the sublime and put his heart and soul into manufacturing great circumstances out of little events. He did not dream, as can be seen, of eluding the family vocation. He wished to devote himself to an attenuated form of spirituality, to a priesthood that would allow him circus riders. Teaching filled the bill: Charles chose to teach German. He defended a thesis on Hans Sachs, adopted the direct method, of which he later called himself the inventor, published, in collaboration with M. Simonnot, a highly esteemed *Deutsches Lesebuch,* and was rapidly promoted: Mâcon, Lyons, Paris. In Paris, he delivered a speech on Prize Day that had the honor of being printed separately: "Mr. Minister of Education, Ladies and Gentlemen, my dear children, you would never guess what I am going to speak about today! About music!" He excelled in occasional verse. He was in the habit of saying at family gatherings: "Louis is the most pious, Auguste the richest, and I the most intelligent." The brothers would laugh; the sisters-in-law would purse their lips. In Mâcon, Charles Schweitzer had married Louise Guillemin, daughter of a Catholic lawyer. She hated her wedding trip. He had carried her off before the end of the meal and rushed her into the train. At the age of seventy, Louise was still talking about the leek salad they had been served at a railway snack-bar: "He took all the white and left me the green." They spent two weeks in Alsace without leaving the table. The brothers told each other scatological jokes in the provincial dialect; from time to time, the pastor would turn to Louise and translate them for her, out of Christian charity. It was not long before an obliging doctor provided her with a certificate exempting her from conjugal intercourse and entitling her to a separate bedroom. She spoke of her headaches, got into the habit of lying down and began to hate noise, passion, enthusiasm, the whole rough, theatrical life of the Schweitzers. That lively and shrewd but cold woman thought straight but inaccurately, because her husband thought accurately but amiss. Because he was credulous and a liar, she doubted everything: "They claim the earth goes round. What do they know about it?" Surrounded by virtuous play-actors, she conceived an aversion for play-acting and virtue. That subtle realist who had strayed into a family of coarse spiritualists became Voltairian out of defiance, without having read Voltaire. Dainty and pudgy, cynical, sprightly, she became a pure negation. With a raising of eyebrows, with an imperceptible smile, she reduced all the grand attitudes to dust, purely for her own sake, without anyone's realizing it. Her negative pride and self-centered rejection consumed her. She saw nobody, being too proud to court favor for first place and too vain to be content with second. "Know how to make people want you," she would say. She was wanted a great deal, then less and less, and, not seeing her, people finally forgot about her. She now almost never got up from her chair or bed. Naturalists and puritans—this combination of virtues is less rare than one thinks —the Schweitzers were fond of crude words which, though belittling the body in very Christian fashion, manifested their broad acceptance of the natural functions. Louise was fond of understatement. She read lots of spicy novels, but it was not so much the plot that interested her as the transparent veils in which it was enveloped: "It's daring, it's well written," she would say with a delicate air. "Gently, mortals, be discreet." That woman of snow thought she would die laughing when she read Adolphe Belot's *Girl of Fire*. She liked to tell stories about wedding-nights which always had an unhappy ending: sometimes the husband, in his brutal haste, would break his wife's neck against the headboard, and sometimes the young bride would be found in the morning, sheltering herself on top of the wardrobe, naked and mad. Louise lived in semidarkness. Charles would enter her room, push open the blinds, light all the lamps; she would put her hand to her eyes and wail: "Charles! You're blinding me!" But her resistance did not exceed the limits of a merely formal opposition: her feeling for Charles was one of fear, of tremendous annoyance, at times too of friendship, provided he did not touch her. She always gave in to him as soon as he started shouting. He fathered four children upon her by surprise: a girl who died in infancy, two boys, and another girl. Out of indifference or respect, he allowed them to be brought up in the Catholic religion. Louise, though a non-believer, made believers of them out of disgust with Protestantism. The two boys sided with their mother; she weaned them away from that bulky father; Charles did not even notice it. The elder, Georges, went to the École Polytechnique; the younger, Emile, became a teacher of German. He intrigues me: I know that he remained a bachelor and that he imitated his father in everything, though he did not love him. Father and son ended by falling out: there were memorable reconciliations. Emile concealed his life; he worshipped his mother and, to the very end, continued to visit her secretly, without notice; he would cover her with kisses and caresses, then start talking about his father, first ironically, then in a rage, and would slam the door behind him when he left. She loved him,

I think, but he frightened her: those two un-
couth, difficult men wearied her. She preferred
Georges, who was never there. Emile died in
1927, mad with solitude: a revolver was found
under his pillow and a hundred pairs of torn
socks and twenty pairs of worn-out shoes in his
trunks.

Anne Marie, the younger daughter, spent her
childhood on a chair. She was taught to be bored,
to sit up straight, to sew. She was gifted: the
family thought it distinguished to leave her gifts
undeveloped; she was radiant: they hid the fact
from her. Those proud, modest bourgeois were
of the opinion that beauty was beyond their
means or below their station; it was all right for
a marquise or a whore. Louise's pride was utterly
barren: for fear of making a fool of herself, she
refused to recognize the most obvious qualities
of her children, her husband, and herself. Charles
was unable to recognize beauty in others: he confused it with health. Ever since his wife's illness,
he had been consoling himself with robust, ideal-
istic ladies who were ruddy and moustached and
who had nothing wrong with them. Fifty years
later, when turning the pages of a family album,
Anne Marie realized that she had been beautiful.

At about the same time that Charles Schweitzer
met Louise Guillemin, a country doctor married
the daughter of a rich landowner from Périgord

and settled down with her on the dreary main street of Thiviers, opposite the pharmacy. The day after the wedding, it was discovered that the father-in-law did not have a penny. Dr. Sartre, outraged, did not speak a word to his wife for forty years. At the table, he expressed himself by signs; she ended by referring to him as "my boarder." Yet he shared her bed and, from time to time, made her pregnant. She gave him two sons and a daughter; these children of silence were named Jean-Baptiste, Joseph and Hélène. Hélène married, late in life, a cavalry officer who went mad. Joseph did his military service in the Zouaves and retired at an early age to the home of his parents. He had no occupation. Caught between the stubborn silence of one parent and the shouting of the other, he developed a stammer and spent his life fighting words. Jean-Baptiste wanted to prepare for the Naval Academy, to see the ocean. In 1904, at Cherbourg, the young naval officer, who was already wasting away with the fevers of Cochin-China, made the acquaintance of Anne Marie Schweitzer, took possession of the big, forlorn girl, married her, begot a child in quick time, me, and sought refuge in death.

Dying is not easy. The intestinal fever rose without haste; there were abatements. Anne Marie nursed him devotedly, but without carrying indecency to the point of loving him. Louise had warned her about married life: after a blood wedding, it was an infinite succession of sacrifices, broken by nocturnal crudities. Following her mother's example, my mother preferred duty to pleasure. She had not known my father well, either before or after marriage, and must have wondered at times why that stranger had chosen to die in her arms. He was taken to a small farm a few miles from Thiviers; his father came to visit him every day in a cart. The sleepless nights and the worry exhausted Anne Marie; her milk dried; I was put out to nurse not far away and I too applied myself to dying, of enteritis and perhaps of resentment. At the age of twenty, without experience or advice, my mother was torn between two unknown moribund creatures. Her marriage of convenience found its truth in sickness and mourning. I benefited from the situation: mothers of the period nursed their babies, and for a long time. Were it not for the luck of that double death-struggle, I would have been exposed to the difficulties of a late weaning. Sick, weaned by force, I was prevented by fever and stupor from feeling the last snip of the scissors that cuts the bonds between mother and child. I sank into a chaotic world full of simple hallucinations and defaced idols. Upon the death of my father, Anne Marie and I awoke from a common nightmare. I got better. But we were victims of a misunderstanding: she returned lovingly to a child she had never really left; I regained consciousness in the lap of a stranger.

Without money or a profession, Anne Marie decided to go back to live with her parents. But my father's insolent decease had displeased the Schweitzers; it looked too much like a repudiation. My mother was deemed guilty of not having foreseen or forestalled it. She had thoughtlessly taken a husband who had not worn well. Everyone behaved perfectly toward the willowy Ariadne who returned to Meudon with a child in her arms. My grandfather had applied for a retirement pension; he went back to teaching without a word of reproach. My grandmother herself was discreet in her triumph. But Anne Marie, chilled with gratitude, sensed the reproach beneath the correct behavior. Families, to be sure, prefer widows to unmarried mothers, but just about. To obtain forgiveness, she gave of herself unstintingly, kept house for her parents in Meudon and then in Paris, became nurse, majordomo, companion, servant, without being able to break down her mother's unspoken annoyance. Louise found it tiresome to prepare the day's menu every morning and examine the accounts every evening, but she disliked anyone's attending to these matters in her place. She let herself be relieved of her obligations, but was irritated at losing her prerogatives. That aging and cynical woman had only one illusion: she thought she was indispensable. The illusion vanished. Louise began to grow jealous of her daughter. Poor Anne Marie: had she been passive, she would have been accused of being a burden; being active, she was suspected of wanting to rule the roost. She needed all her courage to avoid the first peril and all her humility to avoid the second. It did not take long for the young widow to become a minor again, a stainless virgin. She was not refused pocket money: they forgot to give her any. She wore out her wardrobe without its occurring to my grandfather to renew it. They barely tolerated her going out alone. When her former friends, most of whom were married, invited her to dinner, she had to apply for permission long in advance and her hosts had to promise to bring her back by ten o'clock. In the middle of the meal, the head of the house would get up from the table to drive her home. Meanwhile, my grandfather would pace up and down his bedroom with his watch in his hand. At the last stroke of ten, he would thunder. Invitations grew rarer, and my mother lost her taste for such costly pleasures.

The death of Jean Baptiste was the big event of my life: it sent my mother back to her chains and gave me freedom.

There is no good father, that's the rule. Don't lay the blame on men but on the bond of paternity, which is rotten. To beget children, nothing better; to *have* them, what iniquity! Had my father lived, he would have lain on me at full length and would have crushed me. As luck had it, he died young. Amidst Aeneas and his fellows who carry their Anchises on their backs, I move from shore to shore, alone and hating those invisible begetters who bestraddle their sons all their life long. I left behind me a young man who did not have time to be my father and who could now be my son. Was it a good thing or a bad? I don't know. But I readily subscribe to the verdict of an eminent psychoanalyst: I have no Superego.

Dying isn't everything: one must die in time. Later, I would have felt guilty; a conscious orphan lays the blame on himself: shocked at the sight of him, his parents have gone off to their home in heaven. As for me, I was delighted: my sad situation commanded respect; I counted my bereavement as one of my virtues. My father had been so gallant as to die in the wrong: my grandmother kept repeating that he had shirked his duties; my grandfather, rightly proud of the Schweitzer longevity, would not hear of anyone's disappearing at the age of thirty. In the light of that suspect decease, he began to doubt that his son-in-law had ever existed, and he finally forgot about him. I did not even have to forget; in slipping away, Jean Baptiste had refused me the pleasure of making his acquaintance. Even now I am surprised at how little I know about him. Yet he loved, he wanted to live, he saw himself dying; that is enough to make a whole man. But no one in my family was able to make me curious about that man. For several years, I was able to see above my head a photograph of a frank-looking little officer with a round, baldish head and a thick moustache. The picture disappeared when my mother remarried. I later inherited some books that had belonged to him: a work by Le Dantec on the future of science, another by Weber entitled *Toward Positivism through Absolute Idealism*. He read bad books, like all his contemporaries. In the margins, I came upon indecipherable scribbles, dead signs of a little illumination that had been alive and dancing at about the time of my birth. That defunct was of so little concern to me that I sold the books. I know him by hearsay, like the Man in the Iron Mask and the Chevalier d'Eon, and what I do know about him never has anything to do with me. Nobody remembered whether he loved me, whether he took me in his arms, whether he looked at his son with his limpid eyes, now eaten by worms. Love's labor's lost. That father is not even a shadow, not even a gaze. We trod the same earth for a while, that is all. Rather than the son of a dead man, I was given to understand that I was a child of miracle. That accounts, beyond a doubt, for my incredible levity. I am not a leader, nor do I aspire to become one. Command, obey, it's all one. The bossiest of men commands in the name of another—his father— and transmits the abstract acts of violence which he puts up with. Never in my life have I given an order without laughing, without making others laugh. It is because I am not consumed by the canker of power: I was not taught obedience.

Whom would I obey? I am shown a young giantess, I am told she's my mother. I myself would take her rather for an elder sister. That virgin who is under surveillance, who is obedient to everyone, I can see very well that she's there to serve me. I love her, but how can I respect her if no one else does? There are three bedrooms in our home: my grandfather's, my grandmother's, and the "children's." The "children" are we: both alike are minors and both alike are supported. But all consideration is for me. A young girl's bed has been put into *my* room. The girl sleeps alone and awakens chastely. I am still sleeping when she hurries to the bathroom to take her "tub." She comes back all dressed. How could I have been born of her? She tells me her troubles, and I listen compassionately. Later, I'll marry her to protect her. I promise her I will: I'll take her hand in mine, my youthful importance will serve her. Does anyone think I'm going to obey her? I am so good as to give in to her requests. Besides, she does not give me orders; she outlines in light words a future which she praises me for being so kind as to bring into being: "My little darling will be very nice, very reasonable. He'll sit still so I can put drops into his nose." I let myself be caught in the trap of these coddling prophecies.

There remained the patriarch. He so resembled God the Father that he was often taken for Him. One day he entered a church by way of the vestry. The priest was threatening the infirm of purpose with the lightning of heaven: "God is here! He sees you!" Suddenly the faithful perceived beneath the pulpit a tall, bearded old man who was looking at them. They fled. At other times, my grandfather would say that they had flung themselves at his knees. He developed a taste for apparitions. In September 1914, he appeared in a movie-house in Arcachon: my mother and I were in the balcony when he asked for light; other gentlemen were playing angel around him and crying "Victory! Victory!" God got up on the stage and read the communiqué from the Marne. When his beard had been black, he had been Jehovah, who, I suspect, was indirectly responsible for Emile's death. This God of wrath gorged on his sons' blood. But I appeared at the end of his long life; his beard had turned white, tobacco had yellowed it; and fatherhood no longer amused him. Had he begotten me, however, I think he would have been unable to keep from oppressing me, out of habit. My luck was to belong to a dead man. A dead man had paid out the few drops of sperm that are the usual cost of a child; I was a fief of the sun, my grandfather could enjoy me without possessing me. I was his "wonder" because he wanted to finish his life as a wonderstruck old man. He chose to regard me as a singular favor of fate, as a gratuitous and always revocable gift. What could he have required of me? My mere presence filled him to overflowing. He was the God of Love with the beard of the Father and the Sacred Heart of the Son. There was a laying on of hands, and I could feel the warmth of his palm on my skull. He would call me his "tiny little one" in a voice quavering with tenderness. His cold eyes would dim with tears. Everybody would exclaim: "That scamp has driven him crazy!" He worshipped me, that was manifest. Did he love me? In so public a passion it's hard for me to distinguish sincerity from artifice. I don't think he displayed much affection for his other grandchildren. It's true that he hardly ever saw them and that they had no need of him, whereas I depended on him for everything: what he worshipped in me was his generosity.

The fact is, he slightly overdid the sublime. He was a man of the nineteenth century who took himself for Victor Hugo, as did so many others, including Victor Hugo himself. This handsome man with the flowing beard who was always waiting for the next opportunity to show off, as the alcoholic is always waiting for the next drink, was the victim of two recently discovered techniques: the art of photography and the art of being a grandfather*. He had the good and bad fortune to be photogenic. The house was filled with photos of him. Since snapshots were not practiced, he had acquired a taste for poses and *tableaux vivants*. Everything was a pretext for him to suspend his gestures, to strike an attitude, to turn to stone. He doted upon those brief moments of eternity in which he became his own statue. Given his taste for *tableaux vivants,* I have retained only some stiff lantern-slide images of him: a forest interior, I am sitting on a tree-trunk, I am five years old; Charles Schweitzer is wearing a Panama hat, a cream-colored flannel suit with black stripes, a white piqué vest with a watch-chain strung across it; his pince-nez are hanging from a silk cord; he bends over me,

* *The Art of Being a Grandfather* is the title of a work by Hugo. (Translator's note)

raises a ringed finger, speaks. All is dark, all is
damp, except his solar beard: he wears his halo
around his chin. I don't know what he's saying.
I was too busy listening to hear. I suppose that
this old, Empire-bred republican was teaching
me my civic duties and relating bourgeois history. There had been kings, emperors; they were
very wicked; they had been driven out; everything was happening for the best. In the late
afternoon, when we went to wait for him on the
road, we would soon recognize him in the crowd
of travelers emerging from the funicular by his
tall figure and dancing-master's walk. As soon
as he saw us, however far away, he would "take
his stance" in obedience to the behests of an invisible photographer: beard flowing in the wind,
body erect, feet at right angles, chest out, arms
wide open. At this signal, I would stop moving,
I would lean forward, I was the runner getting
set, the little birdy about to spring from the
camera. We would remain for a few moments
face to face, a pretty chinaware group; then I
would dash forward, laden with fruit and flowers,
with my grandfather's happiness, I would go
hurtling against his knees, pretending to be out
of breath. He would lift me from the ground,
raise me to the skies, at arm's length, bring me
down upon his heart, murmuring: "My precious!" That was the second figure, which the
passers-by could not fail to notice. We would put

on a full act with a hundred varied sketches: the flirtation, the quickly dispelled misunderstandings, the good-humored teasing and pretty scolding, the lover's chagrin, the tender pretense of mystery, and the passion; we would imagine our love being thwarted so as to have the joy of triumphing in the end. I was at times imperious, but caprices could not mask my exquisite sensibility. He would display the sublime, artless vanity that befits grandfathers, the blindness, the guilty weaknesses recommended by Hugo. If I had been put on bread and water, he would have brought me jam; but the two terrorized women took care not to put me on such a diet. And besides, I was a good child: I found my role so becoming that I did not step out of it. Actually, my father's early retirement had left me with a most incomplete "Oedipus complex." No Superego, granted. But no aggressiveness either. My mother was mine; no one challenged my peaceful possession of her. I knew nothing of violence and hatred; I was spared the hard apprenticeship of jealousy. Not having been bruised by its sharp angles, I knew reality only by its bright unsubstantiality. Against whom, against what, would I have rebelled? Never had someone else's whim claimed to be my law.

I nicely allow my mother to put drops into my nose, to put my shoes on my feet, to brush and wash me, to dress and undress me, to rub me down and tidy me up; I know nothing more amusing than to play at being good. I never cry, I hardly laugh, I don't make noise. At the age of four, I was caught salting the jam: out of love of knowledge, I suppose, rather than out of naughtiness; in any case, that is the only crime I can remember. On Sunday, the two ladies sometimes go to Mass, to hear good music, a well-known organist. Neither of them is a practicing Catholic, but the faith of others inclines them to musical ecstasy. They believe in God long enough to enjoy a toccata. Those moments of high spirituality delight me: everyone looks as if he were sleeping, now is the time to show what I can do. Kneeling on the prayer-stool, I change into a statue; I must not even move a toe; I look straight ahead, without blinking, until tears roll down my cheeks. Naturally, I engage in a titanic fight against cramp, but I am sure of winning. I am so conscious of my force that I do not hesitate to arouse within me the most criminal temptations just in order to give myself the pleasure of rejecting them: what if I stood up and yelled "Boom!"? What if I climbed up the column to make peepee in the holy-water basin? These terrible possibilities will make my mother's congratulations after church all the more precious. But I lie to myself; I pretend to be in danger so as to heighten my glory. Not for a

moment were the temptations giddying; I am far
too afraid of creating a scandal. If I want to
astound people, it's by my virtues. These easy
victories convince me that I have a good character; I have only to give it free play to be
showered with praise. Wicked desires and wicked
thoughts, when there are any, come from the outside; no sooner do they enter me than they wilt
and fade: I am bad soil for evil. Virtuous for the
fun of it, never do I force or constrain myself:
I invent. I have the lordly freedom of the actor
who holds his audience spellbound and keeps re-
fining his role. I am adored, hence I am adorable.
What can be more simple, since the world is well
made? I am told that I am good-looking, I believe it. For some time my right eye has had a
white speck that will make me half-blind and
wall-eyed, but this is not yet apparent. Dozens
of photos are taken of me, and my mother retouches them with colored pencils. In one of them
which has survived, I am pink and blond, with
curls; I am round-cheeked, and my expression
displays a kindly deference toward the established order; my mouth is puffed with hypo-
critical arrogance: I know my worth.

It is not enough for my character to be good;
it must also be prophetic: truth flows from the
mouth of babes and sucklings. Still close to
nature, they are cousins of the wind and the sea:

their stammerings offer broad and vague teachings to him who can hear them. My grandfather had crossed Lake Geneva with Henri Bergson: "I was wild with enthusiasm," he would say. "I hadn't eyes enough to contemplate the sparkling crests, to follow the shimmering of the water. But Bergson sat on his valise and never once looked up." He would conclude from this incident that poetic meditation was preferable to philosophy. He meditated on me: sitting in a deck-chair in the garden, a glass of beer within arm's reach, he would watch me jump and run about; he would look for wisdom in my jumbled talk, and he would find it. I later laughed at this folly; I'm sorry I did; it was the working of death. Charles fought anguish with ecstasy. He admired in me the admirable fruit of the earth so as to convince himself that all is good, even our shabby end. He went to seek the nature which was preparing to take him back; he sought it on the summits, in the waves, amidst the stars, at the origin of my young life, so as to be able to embrace it in its entirety and accept all of it, including the grave that was being dug for him. It was not Truth, but *his* death that spoke to him through my mouth. It is not surprising that the insipid happiness of my early years sometimes had a funereal taste. I owed my freedom to a timely death, my importance to a very expected decease. But what of it! All the Pythia are dead creatures; everyone knows that. All children are mirrors of death.

And besides, my grandfather takes pleasure in being a pain in the ass to his sons. That terrible father has spent his life crushing them. They enter on tiptoe and surprise him at a child's knees: enough to break one's heart! In the struggle between generations, children and old people often join forces: the former pronounce the oracles; the latter puzzle them out. Nature speaks, and experience translates: adults have only to keep their traps shut. Failing a child, one can take a poodle: last year, at the dogs' cemetery, I recognized my grandfather's maxims in the trembling discourse that runs from grave to grave: dogs know how to love; they are gentler than human beings, more faithful; they have tact, a flawless instinct that enables them to recognize Good, to distinguish the good from the wicked. "Polonius," said one unconsoled mistress, "you are better than I. You would not have survived me. I survive you." An American friend was with me. With a burst of indignation, he kicked a cement dog and broke its ear. He was right: when one loves children and animals *too much*, one loves them against human beings.

So I'm a promising poodle; I prophesy. I make childish remarks, they are remembered, they are repeated to me. I learn to make others. I make grown-up remarks. I know how to say things "beyond my years" without meaning to. These remarks are poems. The recipe is simple: you must trust to the Devil, to chance, to emptiness, you borrow whole sentences from grown-ups, you string them together and repeat them without understanding them. In short, I pronounce true oracles, and each adult interprets them as he wishes. The Good is born in the depths of my heart, the True in the young darkness of my Understanding. I admire myself on trust: my words and gestures happen to have a quality that escapes me and that is immediately apparent to grown-ups. It doesn't matter! I'll offer them unfailingly the delicate pleasure that is denied me. My clowning dons the cloak of generosity: poor people were grieved at not having a child; moved to pity, I drew myself out of nothingness in a burst of altruism and assumed the disguise of childhood so as to give them the illusion of having a son. My mother and grandmother often request me to repeat the act of eminent kindness that gave birth to me. They gratify Charles Schweitzer's idiosyncrasies, his fondness for dramatic outbursts. They arrange surprises for him. They hide me behind a piece of furniture. I hold my breath. The women leave the room or pretend to have forgotten about me. I annihilate myself. My grandfather enters the rooms, weary and gloomy, as he would be if I did not exist. Suddenly I come out from my hiding-place, I do him the favor of being born. He sees me, joins in the game, changes expression, and raises his arms to heaven: I fill him to overflowing with my presence. In a word, I give myself; I give myself always and everywhere; I give everything. I have only to push a door to have—I too—the feeling of appearing on the scene. I place my blocks on top of each other, I turn out my mudpies, I yell. Someone comes and exclaims. I've made one more person happy. Meals, sleep, and precautions against bad weather are the high points and chief obligations of a completely ceremonious life. I eat in public, like a king: if I eat *well*, I am congratulated; my grandmother herself cries out: "What a good boy to be hungry!"

I keep creating myself; I am the giver and the gift. If my father were alive, I would know my rights and my duties. He is dead, and I am unaware of them. I have no rights, since love heaps blessings upon me; I have no duties, since I give out of love. Only one mandate: to please; everything for show. What a riot of generosity in our family! My grandfather supports me and I make him happy; my mother devotes herself to all of us. When I think of it now, only that devotion seems true to me, but we tended to overlook it. No matter: our life is only a succession of

ceremonies, and we spend our time showering
each other with tribute. I respect the adults on
the condition that they idolize me. I am frank,
open, gentle as a girl. My thoughts are quite
proper. I trust people. Everybody is good since
everybody is content. I regard society as a strict
hierarchy of merits and powers. Those at the
top of the scale give all they possess to those below them. I am careful, however, not to place myself on the highest level: I am not unaware that
it is reserved for the severe and well-meaning persons who are responsible for the order that pre-
vails. I remain on a little marginal perch not far
from them, and my radiance extends from the top
of the scale to the bottom. In short, I make it my
business to stand aside from the secular power:
neither below nor above, but elsewhere. I, the
grandson of a clerk, am likewise a clerk, even in
childhood; I have the unction of princes of the
Church, a priestly playfulness. I treat inferiors as
equals: this is a pious lie which I tell them in order
to make them happy and by which it is right and
proper that they be taken in, up to a certain point.
To my maid, to the postman, to my dog, I speak
in a patient and sober voice. There are poor people in this orderly world. There are also freaks of
nature, Siamese twins, railway accidents: those
anomalies are nobody's fault. The worthy poor
do not realize that their function is to exercise
our generosity. They are the uncomplaining poor;

they hug the walls. I spring forward, I slip a small coin into their hand and, most important, I present them with a fine equalitarian smile. I find they look stupid, and I do not like to touch them, but I force myself to: it is an ordeal; and besides, they *must* love me, that love will beautify their lives. I know that they lack necessities, and I take pleasure in being their superfluity. Besides, whatever their poverty, they will never suffer as much as my grandfather did: when he was little, he would get up before dawn and dress in the dark; in winter, he had to break the ice in the water jug in order to wash. Happily, things have since been put to rights. My grandfather believes in Progress; so do I: Progress, that long, steep path which leads to me.

It was Paradise. Every morning I woke up dazed with joy, astounded at the unheard-of luck of having been born into the most united family in the finest country in the world. People who were discontented shocked me. What could they complain about? They were rebels. I was extremely worried about my grandmother in particular: it pained me to note that she didn't admire me sufficiently. In point of fact, Louise had seen through me. She openly found fault with me for the hamming with which she dared not reproach her husband: I was a buffoon, a clown, a humbug; she ordered me to stop "smirking and smiling." I was all the more indignant in that I suspected her of belittling my grandfather too: she was "the Spirit that always negates." I would *answer back*; she would demand an apology. Sure of being backed up, I would refuse. My grandfather would seize the opportunity to show his weakness; he would side with me against his wife, who would stand up, outraged, and go lock herself up in her room. My mother, anxiously fearing my grandmother's rancor, would speak in a low voice and humbly lay the blame on my grandfather, who would shrug and withdraw to his study. Finally, she would beg me to go and ask my grandmother to forgive me. I enjoyed my power: I was Saint Michael and I had laid low the Evil Spirit. In the end, I would go and apologize casually. Apart from that, of course, I adored her: *since* she was my grandmother. It had been suggested that I call her Mamie and call the head of the household by his Alsatian name, Karl. Karl and Mamie, that sounded better than Romeo and Juliet, than Philemon and Baucis. My mother would repeat to me a hundred times a day, not without a purpose: "Karlémami are waiting for us; Karlémami will be pleased; Karlémami . . . ," conjuring up, by the intimate union of those four syllables, the perfect harmony of the persons. I was only half taken in, but I managed to seem to be entirely: first of all, to myself. The word cast its shadow on the thing;

through Karlémami I could maintain the flawless unity of the family and transfer a good part of Charles' merits to Louise. Suspect and sinful, always on the verge of erring, my grandmother was held back by the arms of angels, by the power of a word.

There are real evildoers: the Prussians, who took Alsace-Lorraine away from us, and all our clocks, except the black marble one which adorns my grandfather's mantel and which, as it happens, was given to him by a group of German pupils; we wonder where they stole it. My family buys me the books of Hansi; they show me the pictures in them. I feel no antipathy for those pink, stocky men who so strongly resemble my Alsatian uncles. My grandfather, who chose France in 1871, goes every now and then to Gunsbach, to Pfaffenhofen, to visit those who remained behind. I am taken along. In the trains, when a German ticket-collector asks him for the tickets, in cafés, when a waiter is slow in coming to take our order, Charles Schweitzer turns crimson with patriotic wrath. The two women clutch his arms: "Charles! How could you? They'll put us out, and then where will you be?" My grandfather raises his voice: "I'd like to see them put me out! I'm at home here!" They push me against him, I look at him appealingly, he calms down. "All right, for the child's sake," he sighs, running his hand over my head with his dry fingers. These scenes set me against him without turning me against the occupants. Moreover, in Gunsbach Charles never fails to lose his temper with his sister-in-law. Several times a week, he throws his napkin on the table and leaves the dining-room, slamming the door behind him. Yet she is not a German. After the meal, we go and moan and sob at his feet; he resists us with a brazen brow. How can I fail to agree with my grandmother's judgment: "Alsace isn't good for him. He oughtn't to go back there so often"? Besides, I'm not so fond of the Alsatians, who treat me without respect, and I'm not so angry that they were taken away from us. It seems that I go too often to the shop of M. Blumenfeld, the Pfaffenhofen grocer, that I disturb him for no reason at all. My aunt Caroline has "remarked on" this to my mother. I am told what she said. For once, Louise and I are accomplices: she detests her husband's family. In Strasbourg, from a hotel room where we are together, I hear high-pitched, lunar sounds. I run to the window: the army! I'm as happy as can be to see Prussia parading by to the sound of that puerile music. I clap my hands. My grandfather has remained in his chair; he grumbles. My mother comes up to me and whispers in my ear that I must get away from the window. I obey, though sulking a bit. I hate the Germans, you bet I do, but without conviction. Besides, Charles can allow himself only a faint touch of chauvinism: in 1911 we left Meudon and moved to Paris, 1 Rue le Goff. He had to retire and, in order to support us, recently founded the Modern Language Institute. The Institute teaches French by the direct method to foreigners who are in Paris for a short stay. The pupils for the most part come from Germany. They pay well. My grandfather puts the gold louis into his jacket pocket without ever counting them. My grandmother, who suffers from insomnia, steals into the hall at night to levy her tithe "on the sly," as she herself tells her daughter. In short, the enemy supports us. A Franco-German war would restore Alsace to us and ruin the Institute; Charles is for maintaining peace. Moreover, there are good Germans who come to our home for lunch: a red-faced, hairy lady-novelist whom Louise calls, with a jealous little laugh, "Charles' Dulcinea;" a bald doctor who backs my mother against doors and tries to kiss her; when she timidly complains, my grandfather exclaims: "You're setting me at loggerheads with everyone!" He shrugs and concludes: "You've been seeing things, my dear daughter," and it's she who feels guilty. All these guests realize that they must go into raptures over my merits. They docilely pet me: which means that in spite of their origins they have an obscure notion of Good. At

the anniversary party to celebrate the founding
of the Institute, there are more than a hundred
guests; light champagne is served; my mother
and Mlle. Moutet play four-handed Bach; in a
blue muslin robe, with stars in my hair and wings
on my back, I made the rounds offering tanger-
ines in a basket; the guests exclaim: "He's really
an angel!" Come now, they're not such bad
people! Of course, we have not given up the idea
of avenging martyred Alsace. Among ourselves,
in a low voice, like our cousins in Gunsbach and
Pfaffenhofen, we kill the Boches with ridicule.
We never get tired of laughing at the girl student
who recently wrote in a French composition:
"Charlotte was stiff with grief on Werther's
grave," or at the young teacher who, in the course
of a dinner, looked at his slice of melon mistrust-
fully and ended by eating it all, including the
seeds and rind. These blunders incline me to indulgence: the Germans are inferior beings who
have the good fortune to be our neighbors; we
shall enlighten them.

A kiss without a moustache, as was said at the
time, is like an egg without salt; I add: and like
Good without Evil, like my life from 1905 to
1914. If one is defined only by opposition, I was
the undefined in person. If love and hate are the
obverse and reverse of the same coin, I loved

nothing and nobody. That was as it should be: one cannot be asked both to hate and to please. Or to please and to love.

Am I therefore a Narcissus? Not even that. Too eager to charm, I forget myself. After all, it doesn't amuse me very much to make mud-pies, to scribble, to perform my natural functions: in order for these to have value in my eyes, at least one grown-up must go into raptures over my products. Happily, there is no lack of applause. Whether the adults listen to my babbling or to *The Art of the Fugue*, they have the same arch smile of enjoyment and complicity. That shows what I am essentially: a cultural asset. Culture permeates me, and I give it off to the family by radiation, just as ponds, in the evening, give off the heat of the day.

I began my life as I shall no doubt end it: amidst books. In my grandfather's study there were books everywhere. It was forbidden to dust them, except once a year, before the beginning of the October term. Though I did not yet know how to read, I already revered those standing stones: upright or leaning over, close together like bricks on the book-shelves or spaced out nobly in lanes of menhirs. I felt that our family's prosperity depended on them. They all looked alike. I disported myself in a tiny sanctuary, surrounded by ancient, heavy-set monuments which had seen me into the world, which would see me out of it, and whose permanence guaranteed me a future as calm as the past. I would touch them secretly to honor my hands with their dust, but I did not quite know what to do with them, and I was a daily witness of ceremonies whose meaning escaped me: my grandfather—who was usually so clumsy that my grandmother buttoned his gloves for him—handled those cultural objects with the dexterity of an officiant. Hundreds of times I saw him get up from his chair with an absent-minded look, walk around his table, cross the room in two strides, take down a volume without hesitating, without giving himself time to choose, leaf through it with a combined movement of his thumb and forefinger as he walked back to his chair, then, as soon as he was seated, open it sharply "to the right page," making it creak like a shoe. At times, I would draw near to observe those boxes which slit open like oysters, and I would see the nudity of their inner organs, pale, fusty leaves, slightly bloated, covered with black veinlets, which drank ink and smelled of mushrooms.

In my grandmother's room, the books lay on their sides. She borrowed them from a circulating library, and I never saw more than two at a time. Those baubles reminded me of New Year goodies because their supple, glistening leaves seemed to have been cut from glossy paper. White, bright, almost new, they served as pretext for mild mysteries. Every Friday, my grandmother would get dressed to go out and would say: "I'm going to return *them*." When she got back, after removing her black hat and her veil, she would take *them* from her muff, and I would wonder, mystified: "Are they the same ones?" She would "cover" them carefully, then, after choosing one of them, would settle down near the window in her easy-chair, put on her spectacles, sigh with bliss and weariness, and lower her eyelids with a subtle, voluptuous smile that I have since seen on the lips of La Gioconda. My mother would remain silent and bid me do likewise. I would think of Mass, death, sleep; I would be filled with a holy stillness. From time to time, Louise would chuckle; she would call over her daughter, point to a line, and the two women would exchange a look of complicity. Nevertheless, I did not care for those too distinguished volumes. They were intruders, and my grandfather did not hide the fact that they were the object of a minor cult, exclusively feminine. On Sundays, having nothing better to do, he would enter his wife's room and stand in front of her without finding anything to say. Everyone would look at him. He would drum on the window-pane, then, not knowing what else to do, would turn to Louise and take her novel from her hands. "Charles!" she would cry furiously, "you're going to lose my place!" He would start reading, with raised eyebrows. Suddenly his forefinger would strike the volume: "I don't get it!" "But how do you expect to?" my grandmother would say. "You open to the middle!" He would end by tossing the book on the table and would leave, shrugging his shoulders.

He was surely right, since he was a professional. I knew he was. He had shown me, on a book-shelf, a series of stout volumes bound in brown cloth. "Those, my boy, were written by grandfather." How proud I felt! I was the grandson of a craftsman who specialized in the making of sacred objects, who was as respectable as an organ-maker, as a tailor for ecclesiastics. I saw him at work. Every year a new edition of the *Deutsches Lesebuch* was brought out. During vacation, the whole family would look forward to receiving the proofs. Charles could not bear being inactive. He would lose his temper just to pass the time. The postman would finally bring some big, soft packages. We would cut the string with scissors. My grandfather would unfold the galleys, spread them out on the dining-room table, and slash them with red strokes. At every printer's error, he would curse to God between his teeth, but he no longer yelled, except when the maid wanted to set the table. Everyone was satisfied. Standing on a chair, I would contemplate with ecstasy those black, blood-streaked lines. Charles Schweitzer let me know that he had a deadly enemy, his Publisher. My grandfather had never known how to count. Thoughtlessly lavish and ostentatiously generous, he ended, much later, by falling a victim to that disease of octogenarians, avarice, which is a consequence of helplessness and the fear of death. At the period I am discussing, it was foreshadowed by a strange distrust: when he received his royalties by money order, he would raise his arms to heaven and cry that they were cutting his throat, or he would go to my grandmother's room and declare grimly: "My publisher's robbing me right and left." I discovered, to my stupefaction, the exploitation of man by man. Without that abomination, which fortunately was limited, the world would have been well made: employers gave, according to their ability to pay, to workers according to their merit. Why did publishers, those vampires, have to spoil things by drinking my poor grandfather's blood? My respect increased for that holy man whose devotion was unrewarded. I was prepared at an early age to regard teaching as a priesthood and literature as a passion.

I did not yet know how to read, but I was pretentious enough to demand to have *my* books.

My grandfather went to the office of his rascal of a publisher and was given *The Tales* of the poet Maurice Bouchor, stories taken from folklore and adapted for children by a man who had kept, as he said, a child's outlook. I wanted to start the ceremonies of appropriation at once. I took the two little volumes, sniffed at them, felt them, and opened them casually "to the right page," making them creak. In vain: I did not have the feeling of ownership. I tried, with no greater success, to treat them like dolls, to rock them, to kiss them, to beat them. On the verge of tears, I finally put them on my mother's lap. She raised her eyes from her sewing: "What would you like me to read to you, darling? The Fairies?" I asked incredulously: "Are the Fairies *in there*?" I knew the story; my mother often told it to me when she washed me, breaking off to rub me down with eau de Cologne or to pick up the soap which had slipped from her hands under the bathtub, and I would listen absently to the story which I knew only too well. I had eyes only for Anne Marie, that young lady who graced my mornings; I had ears only for that voice of hers which wavered with servitude; I took pleasure in her unfinished sentences, in her faltering words, in her sudden assurance, which quickly weakened and fled, petering out melodiously, and which, after a silence, came together again. The story was only an added attraction: it was what linked

up her soliloquies. While she spoke, we were
alone and clandestine, far from men, gods, and
priests, two does in a wood, with those other
does, the Fairies. I simply could not believe that
someone had composed a whole book to tell about
that episode of our profane life, which smelled
of soap and eau de Cologne.

Anne Marie sat me down opposite her, on my
little chair. She bent forward, lowered her eyelids, fell asleep. From that statue-like face came
a plaster voice. I was bewildered: who was telling what and to whom? My mother had gone
off: not a smile, not a sign of complicity, I was
in exile. And besides, I didn't recognize her
speech. Where had she got that assurance? A
moment later, I realized: it was the book that
was speaking. Frightening sentences emerged
from it: they were real centipedes, they swarmed
with syllables and letters, stretched their diph-
thongs, made the double consonants vibrate. Singing, nasal, broken by pauses and sighs, rich in
unknown words, they were enchanted with themselves and their meanderings without bothering
about me. Sometimes they disappeared before
I was able to understand them; at other times I
understood in advance; and they continued to
roll nobly to their end without sparing me a single
comma. That discourse was certainly not meant
for me. As for the story, it had got dressed up:

the woodcutter, his wife and their daughters, the fairies, all these little people, our fellow creatures, had taken on majesty. Their rags were spoken of with magnificence; the words colored the things, transforming actions into rites and events into ceremonies. Someone began to ask questions: my grandfather's publisher, who specialized in schoolbooks, lost no opportunity to exercise the young reader's intelligence. It seemed to me that a child was being questioned: What would he have done in the woodcutter's place? Which of the two sisters did he prefer? Why? Did he approve of Babette's punishment? But that child was not quite I, and I was afraid to answer. Nevertheless, I did. My weak voice faded, and I felt myself becoming someone else. Anne Marie, with her blind, extra-lucid look, was also someone else. It seemed to me that I was the child of all mothers, that she was the mother of all children. When she stopped reading, I grabbed the books from her and carried them off under my arm without saying thank you.

After a while, I took pleasure in that sudden lift which took me out of myself. Maurice Bouchor treated children with the universal solicitude that department store section managers display for lady-customers. That flattered me. I came to prefer pre-fabricated stories to improvised ones. I grew sensitive to the rigorous succession of the words. At each reading, they returned, always the same and in the same order. I awaited them. In Anne Marie's stories, the characters lived as best they could, as she herself did. They now acquired destinies. I was at Mass: I witnessed the eternal recurrence of names and events.

I then became jealous of my mother and resolved to take her role away. I got my hands on a work entitled *Tribulations of a Chinese in China* and went off with it to a store-room. There, perched on a cot, I pretended to read. My eyes followed the black signs without skipping a single one, and I told myself a story aloud, being careful to utter all the syllables. I was taken by surprise—or saw to it that I was—a great fuss was made, and the family decided that it was time to teach me the alphabet. I was as zealous as a catechumen. I went so far as to give myself private lessons. I would climb up on my cot with Hector Malot's *No Family,* which I knew by heart, and, half reciting, half deciphering, I went through every page of it, one after the other. When the last page was turned, I knew how to read.

I was wild with joy. They were mine, those dried voices in their little herbals, those voices which my grandfather brought back to life with his gaze, which he heard and which I did not hear!

I was going to listen to them, to fill myself with
ceremonious discourse, I would know everything!
I was allowed to browse in the library and I took
man's wisdom by storm. That was what made me.
I later heard anti-Semites reproach Jews any
number of times with not knowing the lessons
and silence of nature; I would answer: "In that
case, I'm more Jewish than they." In vain would
I seek within me the prickly memories and sweet
unreason of a country childhood. I never tilled
the soil or hunted for nests. I did not gather
herbs or throw stones at birds. But books were
my birds and my nests, my household pets, my
barn and my countryside. The library was the
world caught in a mirror. It had the world's infinite thickness, its variety. I launched out into
incredible adventures. I had to climb up on chairs,
on tables, at the risk of causing avalanches that
would have buried me. The works on the top
shelf remained out of reach for a long time.
Others were taken away from me as soon as I
discovered them. Still others hid from me: I had
taken them down, I had started to read them, I
thought I had put them back in the right place.
It would take a week to find them. There were
horrible encounters. I would open an album, I
would come upon a colored plate. Hideous insects
would swarm before my eyes. Lying on the rug,
I undertook fruitless voyages through Fonten-
elle, Aristophanes, Rabelais: the sentences would

resist me the way objects resist. They had to be observed, encircled, I would pretend to move away and then suddenly come back so as to catch them off guard. Most of the time, they kept their secret. I would be La Pérouse, Magellan, Vasco da Gama; I would discover strange natives: "Heauton Timoroumenos" in a translation of Terence in alexandrines, "idiosyncrasy" in a work of comparative literature. Apocope, Chiasmus, Paragon, a hundred other distant, impenetrable Kaffirs would spring out at the turn of a page, and their appearance alone would throw the whole paragraph off balance. It was not until ten or fifteen years later that I learned the meaning of those hard, black words, and even now they retain their opacity: that is the humus of memory.

The library contained little other than the major French and German classics. There were grammars, too, a few novels, de Maupassant's *Selected Stories*, some art books—a *Rubens*, a *Van Dyck*, a *Dürer*, a *Rembrandt*—which my grandfather's pupils had given him as New Year gifts. A lean universe. But for me the Larousse Encyclopedia took the place of everything: I would pick a volume at random, behind the desk, on the next-to-last shelf, A-Bello, Belloc-Ch or Ci-D, Mele-Po or Pr-Z (these associations of syllables had become proper names which designated sectors of universal knowledge: there was

the Ci-D region, the Pr-Z region, with their
flora and fauna, cities, great men, and battles);
I would set it down laboriously on my grandfather's blotter, I would open it. There I would
take real birds from their nests, would chase
real butterflies that alighted on real flowers. Men
and animals were there *in person*: the engravings
were their bodies, the texts were their souls, their
individual essence. Beyond the walls, one encountered rough sketches which more or less ap-
proximated the archetypes without achieving
their perfection: the monkeys in the zoo were less
monkey, the men in the Luxembourg Gardens
were less man. In Platonic fashion, I went from
knowledge to its subject. I found more reality
in the idea than in the thing because it was given
to me first and because it was given as a thing.
It was in books that I encountered the universe:
assimilated, classified, labeled, pondered, still
formidable; and I confused the disorder of my
bookish experiences with the random course of
real events. From that came the idealism which it
took me thirty years to shake off.

Daily life was cloudless. We consorted with
sedate people who spoke out loud and clear, who
based their certitudes on sound principles, on
the Wisdom of Nations, and who deigned to distinguish themselves from the common herd only
by a certain affectedness of soul to which I was

quite accustomed. No sooner did they express an opinion than its crystal clarity convinced me how obviously true it was. When they wished to justify their actions, they gave reasons which were so dull that they could not fail to be true. Their scruples, which they set forth with self-satisfaction, edified rather than disturbed me; they were false conflicts, resolved in advance and always the same. Their errors, when they did recognize them, lay lightly on their conscience. Haste or legitimate, though no doubt exaggerated, annoyance had clouded their judgment. Luckily they had realized it in time. The errors of those who were not present, which were more serious, were never unforgivable. There was no backbiting in our circle; we simply recognized, with deep regret, defects of character. I listened, I understood, I approved. I found these comments reassuring, and rightly, since they were meant to reassure: nothing is irremediable and, fundamentally, nothing moves; vain surface disturbances must not hide from us the deathlike calm which is our lot.

Our visitors would leave, I would be left alone, I would escape from that graveyard of banalities and go back to life, to the wildness in books. I had only to open one to rediscover the inhuman, restless thinking whose pomp and darkness were beyond my understanding, which jumped from

one idea to the other so quickly that I would lose
my grip on it a dozen times a page and let it slip
by, feeling lost and bewildered. I was involved in
happenings which my grandfather would certainly have deemed unlikely and which nevertheless had the blazing truth of the written word.
The characters would loom up without warning,
would love and quarrel and cut each other's
throat; the survivor would be consumed with grief
and would end in the grave in order to join the
friend or gentle sweetheart he had just murdered.
What was to be done? Was I, like grown-ups,
supposed to blame, to congratulate, to absolve?
But these odd characters did not at all seem to
be guided by our principles, and their motives,
even when these were given, escaped me. Brutus
kills his son; Mateo Falcone does likewise. This
practice therefore seemed rather common. Yet no
one that I knew had resorted to it. In Meudon,
my grandfather had quarreled with my uncle
Emile, and I had heard them shouting in the
garden. Nevertheless, he did not seem to have
dreamed of killing him. What did he think of
fathers who did away with their children? As for
me, I refrained from passing judgment. My life
was not in danger since I was an orphan, and
those flashy murders amused me somewhat, but
in the accounts of them I felt an approbation that
confused me. I had to make a great effort not to
spit on the engraving that showed the helmeted

Horace running after poor Camille with a drawn sword. Karl would sometimes hum:

> *No closer kin can e'er be found*
> *Than a brother and his sister . . .*

That bothered me: if by chance I were given a sister, would she have been closer to me than Anne Marie? Than Karlémami? Then I would have been her lover. Lover was a mysterious word that I often came upon in Corneille's tragedies. Lovers kiss and promise to sleep in the same bed (a strange custom: why not in twin beds, like my mother and me?). I knew nothing more, but beneath the luminous surface of the idea I sensed a hairy mass. In any case, had I been a brother I would have been incestuous. I would dream that I was. A displacement? A camouflaging of forbidden feelings? That's quite possible. I had an elder sister, my mother, and I wanted a younger sister. Even now—1963— that's the only family relationship which moves me*. I have committed the grave mistake of often

* At about the age of ten, I read with great pleasure *Les Transatlantiques*, which tells about a little American boy and his sister, both of them very innocent. I identified myself with the boy, and through him loved Biddy, the little girl. I thought for a long time of writing a story about two lost children who were discreetly incestuous. Traces of this fantasy can be found in my writings: Orestes and Electra in *The Flies*, Boris and Ivich in *The Paths of Freedom*, Frantz and Leni in *Altona*. The last-named are the only ones who go the whole way. What attracted me about this family bond was not so much the amorous temptation as the taboo against making love: fire and ice, mingled delight and frustration; I liked incest if it remained platonic.

seeking in women the sister who never was: my suit was rejected and I had to pay the costs. Nevertheless, in writing these lines I relive the anger I felt toward the murderer of Camille. It is so fresh and vivid that I wonder whether Horace's crime is not one of the sources of my anti-militarism: military men kill their sisters. I'd have taught that bully of a soldier a thing or two! To begin with, off with his head! Up against the wall with him! I turned the page. My error was demonstrated to me in black and white: the sororicide had to be *acquitted*. For some moments, I fumed, I stamped my hoof like a bull that has been tricked. And then, I hurriedly smothered my wrath. That's how things were, I had to make the best of it: I was too young. I had completely misunderstood; the necessity of that acquittal was, as it happened, established by the many alexandrines that had been unclear to me or that I had impatiently skipped. I liked this uncertainty and the fact that the story eluded me on all sides. That added to the magic. I reread the last pages of *Madame Bovary* twenty times and ended by knowing whole paragraphs by heart without understanding any more about the poor widower's behavior. He found some letters. Was that a reason for letting his beard grow? He looked at Rodolphe gloomily, that meant he bore him ill will—but actually *why*? And why did he say to him: "I bear you no ill will"? Why did Rodolphe find him "comic and somewhat base"? Then Charles Bovary died: of grief? of illness? And why did the doctor open him up, since it was all over? I loved that tough resistance which I was unable to overcome. Mystified and weary, I relished the ambiguous delight of understanding without understanding: that was the density of the world. I found the human heart, of which my grandfather was fond of speaking, insipid and hollow, except in books. My moods were conditioned by giddying names that threw me into states of terror or melancholy, the reasons for which escaped me. I would say "Charbovary" and would see, nowhere, a tall, bearded man in rags walking in a walled yard: it was unbearable. At the root of those anxious delights was the combination of two conflicting fears. I was afraid of falling head first into a fabulous universe and of wandering about in it in the company of Horace and Charbovary without hope of getting back to the Rue le Goff, Karlémami, and my mother. And, on the other hand, I sensed that those processions of sentences had meanings for grown-up readers which escaped me. I let venomous words enter my head, words infinitely richer than I realized; a foreign force recomposed within me, by means of discourse, stories about madmen that didn't concern me, a dreadful sorrow, the ruin of a life: wasn't I going to be infected, to die poisoned? Absorbing the Word, absorbed by the picture, I was actually saved by the incompatibility of those two simultaneous perils. At nightfall, lost in a jungle of words, jumping at the slightest sound, taking the creaking of the floor for interjections, I felt I was discovering language in the state of nature, without human beings. With what cowardly relief, with what disappointment I returned to the family small talk when my mother entered and put on the light, crying: "My poor darling, you're straining your eyes!" Drawn and haggard, I would spring to my feet, cry out, and run to her; I was putting on my act. But even in that childhood regained, questions kept plaguing me: *what* do books talk about, who writes them, why? I unbosomed myself to my grandfather, who, after due reflection, decided it was time to enlighten me, and he did, in such a way that he left his mark on me.

For years my grandfather rode me up and down on his leg and sang: "Riding upon my bidet, when it trots it leaves a fart," and I would laugh with shame. This time, he didn't sing; he sat me down on his lap and looked me deep in the eyes: "I am a man," he repeated in a public voice, "and nothing human is alien to me." He exaggerated a great deal; as Plato did with the poet, Charles drove the engineer, the merchant, and probably the officer out of his Republic.

Factories spoiled the landscape for him. As for the pure sciences, he appreciated only their purity. At Guérigny, where we would spend the second half of July, my uncle Georges would take us to visit the foundries. It would be hot; rough, half-dressed men would jostle us. Deafened by the tremendous noise, I was both frightened to death and bored. My grandfather would whistle as he watched the casting, out of politeness, but his expression remained blank. In Auvergne, on the other hand, in the month of August, he would roam the villages, stand in front of old structures, tap the bricks with the end of his cane: "What you see there, my boy," he would say with animation, "is a Gallo-Roman wall." He also appreciated religious architecture, and though he loathed papists, he never failed to enter a church if it was Gothic; as for Romanesque, that depended on his mood. He hardly ever went to concerts any more, though he had gone in the past. He liked Beethoven, his richness, his full orchestra; Bach too, but without relish. Occasionally he would go to the piano and, without sitting down, would strike a few chords with his stiff fingers. My grandmother would say, with a pinched smile: "Charles is composing." His sons, particularly Georges, had become good performers who loathed Beethoven and cared only for chamber music. My grandfather did not mind these differences of taste; he would say with a kindly air: "The Schweitzers are born musicians." A week after I was born, as I seemed to be amused by the tinkling of a spoon, he had decreed that I had a good ear.

Stained glass windows, flying buttresses, sculpted portals, chorals, crucifixions carved in wood or stone, Meditations in verse and poetic Harmonies: these Humanities led us straight to the Divine, all the more in that added to them were the beauties of nature. The works of God and the great achievements of man were shaped by one and the same impulse; the same rainbow shone in the spray of waterfalls, shimmered between the lines of Flaubert, gleamed in the chiaroscuro of Rembrandt: it was the Spirit. The Spirit spoke to God about Men; to Men it bore witness to God. My grandfather saw in Beauty the carnal presence of Truth and the source of the noblest grandeur. In certain exceptional circumstances—when a storm broke on a mountain, when Victor Hugo was inspired—one could attain that Sublime Point where the Good, the True and the Beautiful blended into one.

I had found my religion: nothing seemed to me more important than a book. I regarded the library as a temple. Grandson of a priest, I lived on the roof of the world, on the sixth floor, perched on the highest branch of the Central

Tree: the trunk was the elevator shaft. I would walk up and down on the balcony; I would lean forward to take a look at the passers-by; through the grill I would greet Lucette Moreau, who was the same age as I and had the same blond curls and juvenile femininity; I would return to the *cella* or the *pronaos*; I never went down from it *in person*: when my mother took me to the Luxembourg Gardens—that is, every day—I would lend my rags to the lowlands, but my glorious body did not leave its perch; I think it's still there. Every man has his natural place; its altitude is determined by neither pride nor value: childhood decides. Mine is a sixth floor in Paris with a view overlooking the roofs. For a long time I suffocated in the valleys; the plains overwhelmed me: I crawled along the planet Mars, the heaviness crushed me. I had only to climb a molehill for joy to come rushing back: I would return to my symbolic sixth floor; there I would once again breathe the rarefied air of belles-lettres; the Universe would rise in tiers at my feet and all things would humbly beg for a name; to name the thing was both to create and take it. Without this fundamental illusion I would never have written.

Today, April 22, 1963, I am correcting this manuscript on the tenth floor of a new building: through the open window I see a cemetery, Paris, the blue hills of Saint Cloud. That shows my obstinacy. Yet everything has changed. Had I wished as a child to deserve this lofty position, my fondness for pigeon-houses would have to be regarded as a result of ambition, of vanity, as a compensation for my shortness. But it's not that; it wasn't a matter of climbing up my sacred tree: I *was* there, I refused to come down from it. It was not a matter of setting myself above human beings: I wanted to live in the ether among the aerial simulacra of Things. Later, far from clinging to balloons, I made every effort to sink: I had to wear leaden soles. With luck, I occasionally happened, on naked sands, to brush against submarine species whose names I had to invent. At other times, nothing doing: an irresistible lightness kept me on the surface. In the end, my altimeter went out of order. I am at times a bottle imp, at others a deep-sea diver, often both together, which is as it should be in our trade. I live in the air out of habit, and I poke about down below without much hope.

Nevertheless, I had to be told about authors. My grandfather told me, tactfully, calmly. He taught me the names of those illustrious men. I would recite the list to myself, from Hesiod to Hugo, without a mistake. They were the Saints and Prophets. Charles Schweitzer said he worshipped them. Yet they bothered him. Their obtrusive presence prevented him from attributing the works of Man directly to the Holy Ghost. He therefore felt a secret preference for the anonymous, for the builders who had had the modesty to keep in the background of their cathedrals, for the countless authors of popular songs. He did not mind Shakespeare, whose identity was not established. Nor Homer, for the same reason. Nor a few others, about whom there was no certainty that they had existed. As for those who had not wished or had been unable to efface the traces of their life, he found excuses, provided they were dead. But he lumped his contemporaries together and condemned them, with the exception of Anatole France, and of Courteline, who amused him. Charles Schweitzer proudly enjoyed the consideration that was shown his great age, his culture, his good looks, his virtues. That Lutheran could not help thinking, very biblically, that the Eternal had blessed his House. At the table, he would sometimes collect his thoughts and conclude off-handedly: "My children, how good it is to have nothing with which to reproach each other." His fits of anger, his majesty, his pride, and his taste for the sublime covered up a timidity of mind that came from his religion, his century, and his academic environment. For that reason he felt a secret aversion for the sacred monsters of his library, out-and-out scoundrels whose books he regarded, in his heart of hearts, as incongruities. I was wrong about that: the reserve which appeared beneath a feigned enthusiasm I took for the severity of a judge; his priesthood raised him above them. In any case, as the minister of the cult would whisper to me, genius is only a loan: it must be merited by great suffering, tested by ordeals that must be accepted modestly and firmly. One ends by hearing voices and writes at their dictation. Between the first Russian revolution and the first world war, fifteen years after Mallarmé's death, when Daniel de Fontanin was discovering Gide's *Fruits of the Earth,* a man of the nineteenth century was foisting upon his grandson ideas that had been current under Louis Philippe. That is how peasant routines are said to be handed down: the fathers work in the fields, leaving the sons with the grandparents. I started off with a handicap of eighty years. Ought I to complain? I don't know: in our bustling societies, delays sometimes give a head start. Be that as it may, I was given that bone to chew and did such a thorough job that I now see the light through it. My grandfather had slyly hoped to disgust me with writers, those intermediaries. He achieved the opposite result: I merged talent with merit. Those fine fellows resembled me: when I behaved properly, when I bravely endured my bumps and bruises, I was entitled to laurels, to a reward; that was childhood. Karl Schweitzer showed me other children who had been able to remain my age all their life. I had no brothers and sisters, no playmates, and they were my first friends. They had loved, had suffered manfully, like the heroes of their novels, and, above all, had triumphed in the end. I conjured up their torments with a somewhat cheerful pity: how pleased those fellows must have been when they felt most unhappy; they would say to themselves: "What luck! Here comes a beautiful verse!"

In my sight, they were not dead; at any rate, not entirely. They had been metamorphosed into books. Corneille was a big, rugged, ruddy fellow who smelled of glue and had a leather back. That severe, unwieldy individual, whose words were hard, had angles that hurt my thighs when I carried him. But no sooner did I open him than he presented me with his engravings, which were as dark and sweet as confidences. Flaubert was a cloth-bound, odorless little thing spotted with freckles. The multiple Victor Hugo was on all the shelves at once. So much for the bodies. As for the souls, they haunted the works. The pages were windows; outside, a face was pressed against the pane, someone was watching me. I pretended not to notice and would continue reading, with my eyes glued to the words beneath the fixed stare of the late Chateaubriand. This uneasiness would not last. The rest of the time I adored my playmates. I ranked them above everything, and when I was told that Charles V had picked up Titian's brush, I was not at all surprised. What of it? That was what princes were made for. Yet I did not respect them. Why should I have praised them for being great? They were only doing their duty. I blamed the others for being lesser. In short, I had got everything wrong and was making the exception the rule. The human race became a small committee surrounded by affectionate animals. In addition, my grandfather treated them too badly for me to be able to take them quite seriously. He had stopped reading since the death of Victor Hugo. When he had nothing else to do, he re-read. But his function was to translate. Deep down in his heart, the author of the *Deutsches Lesebuch* regarded world literature as his raw material. By classifying authors in order of merit, he was paying lip-service; this surface hierarchy ill concealed his preferences, which were utilitarian: de Maupassant provided the best translation material for his German pupils; Goethe, beating Gottfried Keller by a nose, could not be equalled for compositions in French. As a humanist, my grandfather held novels in low esteem; as a teacher, he valued them because of their vocabulary. He ended by reading only selected passages, and I saw him, some years later, enjoy an extract from *Madame Bovary* in Mironneau's *Readings* when the com-

plete Flaubert had been awaiting his pleasure
for twenty years. I felt that he lived on the dead,
which to some degree complicated my relations
with them. Under the pretext of worshipping
them, he kept them in chains and did not refrain
from cutting them up in order to carry them
more conveniently from one language to another. I discovered at one and the same time their
grandeur and their wretchedness. Mérimée, un-
luckily for him, was suitable for the Intermediate
Course; he consequently led a double life. On
the fourth shelf of the library, *Columba* was a
dainty, hundred-winged dove, glossy, available
and systematically ignored; no gaze ever de-
flowered her; but on the bottom shelf, that same
virgin was imprisoned in a dirty, smelly little
brown book; neither the story nor the language
had changed, but there were notes in German and
a vocabulary; I learned, in addition—the greatest
scandal since the rape of Alsace-Lorraine—that
it had been published in Berlin. Twice a week,
my grandfather put this book into his brief-case.
He had covered it with stains, burns, red mark-
ings, and I hated it. It was Mérimée humiliated.
Merely to open it bored me to death; each syllable was detached from the one preceding and
following it, just as when my grandfather spoke
at the Institute. Printed in Germany, meant
to be read by Germans, what were those familiar
yet unrecognizable signs if not a counterfeiting

of French words? Another espionage affair! One had only to scratch them to find German vocables lurking beneath their Gallic disguise. I began to wonder whether there were not two Colombas, one true and wild, the other false and didactic, just as there were two Isoldes.

The tribulations of my friends convinced me that I was their equal. I possessed neither their gifts nor their merits, and I was not yet planning to be a writer, but as the grandson of a priest I was superior to them by birth. No doubt I was dedicated; not to their torments, which were always somewhat shocking, but to some priesthood. I would be a sentinel of culture, like Charles Schweitzer. And besides, I was alive, and very active. I did not yet know how to cut the dead into pieces, but I did subject them to my whims. I would take them in my arms, carry them, put them on the floor, open them, shut them, draw them from nothingness, and thrust them back into it. Those garbled figures were my dolls, and I pitied that wretched, paralyzed survival which was called immortality. My grandfather encouraged these familiarities: all children are inspired; they have nothing to envy poets, who are just children. I was mad about Courteline; I would follow the cook into the kitchen to read her *Theodore Looks for the Matches*. The family was amused at my infatuation; they very carefully

developed it; they made my passion known. One
day, my grandfather said to me casually:
"Courteline must be a decent sort of chap. If
you're so fond of him, why not write to him?" I
did write. Charles Schweitzer guided my pen and
decided to leave several spelling mistakes in my
letter. Some newspapers published it a few years
ago, and I reread it with a certain irritation. I
took leave of him with the words "your future
friend," which seemed to me quite natural. Voltaire and Corneille were familiar acquaintances;
how could a *living* writer refuse my friendship?
Courteline did refuse it, and rightly: in writing
to the grandson, he would have fallen in with the
grandfather. At the time, we judged his silence
severely. "I recognize," said Charles, "that he has
a lot of work, but, deuce take it, one answers a
child's letter."

Even now I still have that minor vice, familiarity. I'm free and easy with the illustrious dead.
I say what I have to say about Baudelaire or
Flaubert without mincing words, and when I'm
chided for doing so, I feel like answering: "Don't
butt into our affairs. Those geniuses of yours belong to me. I've held them in my hands, I've
loved them passionately, with all due reverence.
Am I going to handle them with kid gloves?"
But I shook off Karl's humanism, that priestly
humanism, when I came to realize that every

man is all of man. How sad cures are: language is disenchanted; stripped of their privileges, the heroes of the pen, my former peers, have returned to the ranks; I mourn for them twice.

What I have just written is false. True. Neither true nor false, like everything written about madmen, about men. I have reported the facts as accurately as my memory permitted me. But to what extent did I believe in my delirium? That's the basic question, and yet I can't tell. I realized later that we can know everything about our attachments except their force, that is, their sincerity. Acts themselves cannot serve as a measuring-rod unless one has proved that they are not gestures, which is not always easy. Consider the following: alone in the midst of grown-ups, I was a miniature adult and read books written for adults. That already sounds false, since, at the same time, I remained a child. I am claiming that I was guilty. That's how it was, and that's that. The fact remains that my hunting and exploration were part of the family play-acting, that the grown-ups were delighted by it, and that I knew it. Yes, I knew it. Each day a wonderful child awoke the books of magic that his grandfather no longer read. I loved beyond my years as one lives beyond one's means: with zeal, with fatigue, at great cost, for the sake of display. No sooner did I open the door of the library than

I was again in the belly of an inert old man: the
desk, the pink blotter with its red and black ink
spots, the ruler, the pot of glue, the stale smell of
tobacco, and, in winter, the glowing of the coal-
stove, the crackling of the mica; it was Karl in
person, reified. That was all that was needed to
put me into a state of grace. I would rush to the
books. Sincerely? What does that mean? How
could I determine—especially after so many
years—the imperceptible and shifting frontier
that separates possession from hamming? I
would lie on my stomach, facing the windows,
with an open book in front of me, a glass of wine-
tinted water at my right, and a slice of bread and
jam on a plate at my left. Even in solitude I was
putting on an act. Karlémamie and Anne Marie
had turned those pages long before I was born;
it was their knowledge that lay open before my
eyes. In the evening, they would question me:
"What did you read? What have you understood?" I knew it, I was pregnant, I would give
birth to a child's comment. To escape from the
grown-ups into reading was the best way of com-
muning with them. Though they were absent,
their future gaze entered me through the back of
my head, emerged from my pupils, and propelled
along the floor the sentences which had been read
a hundred times and which I was reading for
the first time. I who was seen saw myself. I saw

myself reading as one listens to oneself talking. Had I changed since the time I pretended to read *The Chinese in China* before knowing the alphabet? No, the game went on. The door would open behind me; someone was coming to see "what I was up to." I faked. I would spring to my feet, put Musset back in his place and, standing on tiptoe, would immediately take down the heavy Corneille. The family measured my passion by my efforts. I would hear, behind me, a dazzled voice whisper: "But it's because he *likes* Corneille!" I didn't like him; the alexandrines discouraged me. Luckily the volume contained in full only his most famous tragedies and gave a synopsis of the others. That was what interested me. "Rodelinde, wife of Pertharite, King of Lombardy, who has been vanquished by Grimoald, is urged by Unulphe to give her hand to the foreign prince . . ." I knew Rodogune, Théodore and Agésilas before the Cid and Cinna. I filled my mouth with ringing names and my heart with sublime sentiments, and I was careful not to get lost in the bonds of kinship. The grown-ups would say: "The child has a thirst for knowledge. He devours the encyclopedia," and I let them say it. But it could hardly be said that I was educating myself. I had discovered that the Larousse contained summaries of plays and novels and I reveled in them.

I liked to please and wanted to steep myself in culture. I would recharge myself with the sacred every day, at times absentmindedly. It was enough to prostrate myself and turn the pages. My friends' works frequently served as prayer mills. At the same time, I had honest-to-goodness pleasures and fears. I would sometimes forget my role and race along at breakneck speed, carried away by a mad whale that was none other than the world. So try to draw conclusions! In any case, I worked over the words; I had to try them out, to decide what they meant. The playing at culture cultivated me in the long run.

However, I also read *real* things: outside of the sanctuary, in our bedroom, or under the diningroom table. I never spoke about them to anyone, and no one, except my mother, ever spoke about them to me. Anne Marie had taken my fake transports seriously. She unbosomed herself to Mamie about her anxiety. My grandmother was a sure ally: "Charles isn't reasonable," she said. "It's he who keeps pushing the child. I've seen him do it. Where will it get him if the child wastes away?" The two women also alluded to overstrain and meningitis. It would have been dangerous and fruitless to attack my grandfather head-on. They went at it in a roundabout way. During one of our walks, Anne Marie

stopped, as if by chance, in front of the news-
stand which is still at the corner of the Boulevard Saint Michel and the Rue Soufflot. Wonderful pictures caught my eye; their garish colors
fascinated me; I asked for them; they were given
to me. The trick came off. I wanted every number of *Cri Cri, The Stunner, Vacation,* Jean de
la Hire's *The Three Boy Scouts* and Arnould
Galopin's *Around the World in an Airplane,*
which appeared in installments every Thursday.
From one Thursday to the next I would think
far more about the Eagle of the Andes, Marcel
Dunot, the iron-fisted boxer, and Christian the
aviator than about my friends Rabelais and de
Vigny. My mother began looking about for
works that would bring me back to childhood. At
first there were "the little pink books," monthly
collections of fairy tales; then, little by little,
*Captain Grant's Children, The Last of the
Mohicans, Nicholas Nickleby, Lavarède's Five
Sous.* I preferred the nonsense of Paul d'Ivoi
to Jules Verne, who was too heavy. But, regardless of author, I adored the works in the Hetzel
series, little theatres whose red cover with gold
tassels represented the curtain; the gilt edges
were the footlights. I owe to those magic boxes
—and not to the balanced sentences of Chateaubriand—my first encounters with Beauty. When
I opened them, I forgot about everything. Was
that reading? No, but it was death by ecstasy.

From my annihilation there immediately sprang up natives-armed with spears, the bush, an explorer with a white helmet. I was *vision,* I poured forth light on the beautiful dark cheeks of Aouda, on Phineas Fogg's sideburns. Freed from himself at last, the little wonder became pure wonderment. Twenty inches from the floor, an unfettered, a perfect happiness was born. The New World seemed at first more disturbing than the Old; there were murder and pillage; blood flowed in torrents. Indians, Hindus, Mohicans, Hottentots carried off the girl, tied up her old father, and swore he would be tortured to death. It was pure Evil. But it appeared on the scene only in order to grovel before Good. Everything would be set to rights in the next chapter. Brave Whites would come and slaughter the savages and release the father, who would rush into his daughter's arms. Only the wicked died—plus a few very minor "good" characters, whose deaths were included among the incidental expenses of the story. Moreover, death itself was asepticized. One fell to the ground, arms outstretched, with a little round hole under the left breast, or, if the rifle had not yet been invented, the guilty were "run through with a sword." I liked that pretty expression; I would imagine that straight white flash, the blade; it sank into the body as into butter and came out at the back; the villain would collapse without losing a drop of blood.

At times, the decease was even laughable, as was that of the Saracen—in, I think, *Roland's God-daughter*—who charged his horse into that of a crusader; the paladin struck out with his sabre and cleft the foe in twain from top to toe; the scene was illustrated by Gustave Doré. How funny it was! The two halves of the body began to fall, describing a semi-circle around each stirrup; the horse reared in amazement. For years I could not see the engraving without laughing till the tears came. At last I had what I needed: an Enemy who was hateful, though, when all was said and done, harmless, since his plans came to naught and even, despite his efforts and diabolical cleverness, served the cause of Good. I noted that the return to order was always accompanied by progress; the heroes were rewarded; they received honors, tokens of admiration, money; thanks to their dauntlessness, a territory had been conquered, a work of art had been protected from the natives and taken to our museums; the girl fell in love with the explorer who had saved her life; it all ended with a marriage. From these magazines and books I derived my most deep-seated phantasmagoria: optimism.

This literature remained clandestine for a long time. Anne Marie did not even have to warn me. Aware of its unworthiness, I said not a word about it to my grandfather. I was slumming, I was taking liberties, I was spending a vacation in a brothel but did not forget that my truth had remained in the temple. What was the point of shocking the priest by an account of my deviations? Karl finally caught me. He lost his temper with the two women, and they, taking advantage of a moment when he was getting his second wind, laid the whole blame on me; I had seen the magazines, the adventure novels; I had longed for them, had craved them, could they refuse me? This clever lie forced him to choose between two alternatives. It was I who was deceiving Colomba with those painted hussies. I, the prophetic child, the young Pythoness, the Eliakim of Belles Lettres, was manifesting a wild bent for infamy. He had to choose: either I did not prophesy or he had to respect my tastes without trying to understand them. Had he been my father, Charles Schweitzer would have burned the lot; being my grandfather, he chose regretful indulgence. That was all I wanted, and I peacefully continued my double life. It has never ended. Even now, I read the "Série Noire"* more readily than I do Wittgenstein.

In my aerial isle, I was the foremost, the incomparable. I dropped to the lowest level when I was subjected to the common rules.

* A series of detective novels and thrillers. (Translator's note.)

My grandfather had decided to enroll me at the Lycée Montaigne. One morning he took me to the principal and vaunted my merits. The only trouble with me was that I was *too* advanced for my age. The principal accepted everything he said. I was assigned to a class, and I assumed I would be with children of my own age. But after the first dictation, my grandfather was hastily summoned by the office. He returned in a fury, took from his briefcase a sorry-looking sheet of paper covered with scrawls and blots and threw it on the table. It was the work I had handed in. His attention had been drawn to the spelling— "*le lapen çovache ême le ten*" (*le lapin sauvage aime le thym*)—and he was given to understand that I belonged in a much lower grade. When my mother saw "*lapen çovache*," she had a fit of giggles; my grandfather stopped her with a terrible look. He began by accusing me of not trying and scolding me for the first time in my life. Then he declared that they had misjudged me. The very next day, he withdrew me from the lycée and quarreled with the principal.

I had not understood what was involved, and my failure had not affected me: I was a child prodigy who was not a good speller, that was all. And besides, I didn't mind returning to my solitude: I liked what was wrong with me. I had lost, without even noticing it, the opportunity to become real. My grandfather engaged M. Liéven, a Paris schoolteacher, to give me private lessons. He came almost every day. My grandfather had bought me a plain little wooden desk with a bench. I would sit on the bench and M. Liéven would walk up and down dictating. He resembled Vincent Auriol, and my grandfather maintained that he was a third-degree mason. "When I say hello to him," he told us, with the frightened repulsion of a good citizen to whom a homosexual is making advances, "he makes the masonic triangle with his thumb on the palm of my hand." I disliked him because he forgot to coddle me. I think he took me, not without reason, for a backward child. He disappeared, I don't remember why. Perhaps he expressed his opinion of me to someone.

We spent some time in Arcachon, and I went to a public school there. My grandfather's democratic principles required this. But he also wanted me to be kept away from the herd. He recommended me to the teacher in the following terms: "My dear colleague, I am committing to your care what is dearest to me." M. Barrault wore a goatee and pince-nez. He came to our cottage for a glass of muscatel and declared that he was flattered by the confidence shown him by a member of the secondary school system. He had me sit at a special desk, next to the rostrum, and during recreation periods kept me with him. This special treatment seemed legitimate to me. What the "sons of the people," my equals, thought of it, I don't know. They probably didn't give a damn. As for me, their turbulence fatigued me and I thought it "distinguished" to be bored at M. Barrault's side while they played prisoners' base.

I had two reasons for respecting my teacher: he had my welfare at heart, and he had a strong breath. Grown-ups should be ugly, wrinkled and unpleasant. When they took me in their arms, I didn't mind having to overcome a slight disgust. This was proof that virtue was not easy. There were simple, petty joys: running, jumping, eating cakes, kissing my mother's soft, sweet-smelling skin. But I attached a higher value to the mixed, bookish pleasure that I took in the company of middle-aged men. The repulsion which they made me feel was part of their prestige; I confused disgust with seriousness. I was pretentious. When M. Barrault bent over me, his breath made me exquisitely uncomfortable. I zealously inhaled the repellent odor of his virtues. One day, I came upon a fresh inscription on the school wall; I drew near and read: "Old man Barrault is a prick." My heart began thumping violently. I stood there utterly stupefied. I was afraid. "Prick" could only be one of the "dirty

words" that swarm in the disreputable areas of
vocabulary and that a well bred child never encounters. It was short and brutal and had the horrible simplicity of rudimentary insects. Merely to
have read it was too much. I forbade myself to
pronounce it, even in a whisper. I didn't want
that cockroach on the wall to jump into my mouth
and change into a loud, evil blast. If I pretended
not to have noticed it, perhaps it would creep
back into a hole in the wall. But when I looked
again, there was the unspeakable appellation:
"Old man Barrault," which frightened me even
more. As for the word "prick," after all, I merely
sensed its meaning. But I knew very well that
my family used the words "old man So-and-so"
only when referring to gardeners, postmen, the
maid's father, in short, the old and poor. Someone saw M. Barrault, the teacher, my grandfather's colleague, as being old and poor. Somewhere, in somebody's head, there lurked that sick
and criminal thought. In whose head? In mine,
perhaps. Didn't the mere reading of the blasphe-
matory inscription make me an accomplice in a
sacrilege? It seemed to me both that some cruel
lunatic was jeering at my politeness, my respect,
my zeal, the pleasure I took every morning in
doffing my cap and saying, "Good morning, Mr.
Teacher," and that I myself was that lunatic,
that the dirty words and evil thoughts swarmed
in my heart. What prevented me, for example,

from yelling at the top of my voice: "That old monkey stinks like a pig?" I murmured: "Old man Barrault stinks," and everything began to whirl. I ran away, crying. The next day, I felt the same deference as usual for M. Barrault, for his celluloid collar and bow tie. But when he bent over my notebook, I turned my head and held my breath.

The following autumn my mother decided to take me to the Poupon Academy. We went up a flight of wooden stairs and entered a classroom. The children sat silently in a semi-circle. At the back of the room, the mothers sat upright, with their backs against the wall, watching the teacher. The primary duty of the poor creatures who taught us was to distribute praise and good marks equally to our class of prodigies. If one of them showed the slightest impatience or appeared too satisfied with a good answer, the Misses Poupon would lose pupils and she would lose her job. We were thirty academicians who never had time to speak to each other. When the session was over, each mother would grimly take hold of her child and rush off with him, without a goodbye. At the end of a semester, my mother withdrew me from the course. Not enough was accomplished. And besides, she finally got tired of feeling the pressure of her neighbors' gazes when it was my turn to be congratulated. Mlle.

Marie Louise, a blond young lady with pince-nez
who taught eight hours a day at Poupon Academy for starvation wages, was willing to give
me private lessons at home. She hid the fact from
the directresses. She would occasionally interrupt
the dictation and sigh heavily. She told me that
she was tired to death, that she was terribly
lonely, that she would have given anything to
have a husband, regardless of who he was. She,
too, finally disappeared. The family claimed that
she didn't teach me anything, but I rather think
that my grandfather found her calamitous. That
just man did not refuse to comfort the wretched,
but he was loath to invite them to his home. It
was high time; Mlle. Marie Louise was demoral-
izing me. I thought salaries were proportionate
to worth, and I was told she was worthy. Then
why was she so badly paid? When one practiced
a profession, one was proud and dignified, happy
to work. Since she had the good fortune to work
eight hours a day, why did she talk about her
life as if it were an incurable sickness? When I
reported her grievances, my grandfather started
laughing. She was too homely for any man to
want her. I didn't laugh. Could a person be born
condemned? In that case, I had been told a lie.
The order of the world concealed intolerable disorders. My anxiety disappeared as soon as she
was dismissed. Charles Schweitzer found me more
seemly teachers. So seemly that I have forgotten

all of them. Until the age of ten, I remained alone between an old man and two women.

My truth, my character, and my name were in the hands of adults. I had learned to see myself through their eyes. I was a child, that monster which they fabricated with their regrets. When they were not present, they left their gaze behind, and it mingled with the light. I would run and jump across that gaze, which preserved my nature as a model grandson, which continued to give me my toys and the universe. My thoughts swam around in my pretty glass globe, in my soul. Everyone could follow their play. Not a shadowy corner. Yet, without words, without shape or consistency, diluted in that innocent transparency, a transparent certainty spoiled everything: I was an impostor. How can one put on an act without knowing that one is acting? The clear, sunny semblances that constituted my role were exposed by a lack of being which I could neither quite understand nor cease to feel. I would turn to the grown-ups, I would ask them to guarantee my merits. In doing so, I sank deeper into the imposture. Condemned to please, I endowed myself with charms that withered on the spot. Everywhere I went, I dragged about my false good nature, my idle importance, on the alert for a new opportunity. When I thought that I had seized it, I would strike a pose only to find once again the hollowness which I was trying to get away from. My grandfather would be dozing, wrapped in his plaid blanket. Under his bushy moustache I would see the pink nakedness of his lips. It was unbearable. Luckily his glasses would slide off. I would rush to pick them up. He would awaken, would lift me in his arms, we would play our big love scene. It was no longer what I had wanted. What *had* I wanted? I would forget everything. I would make my nest in the thicket of his beard. I would go into the kitchen, would declare that I wanted to dry the salad. There would be cries and giggles: "No, darling, not like that. Squeeze your little hand tighter. That's right! Marie, help him. But he's doing it very well." I was a fake child, I was holding a fake salad-washer. I could feel my acts changing into gestures. Play-acting robbed me of the world and of human beings. I saw only roles and props. Serving the activities of adults in a spirit of buffoonery, how could I have taken their worries seriously? I adapted myself to their intentions with a virtuous eagerness that kept me from sharing their purposes. A stranger to the needs, hopes, and pleasures of the species, I squandered myself coldly in order to charm it. It was my audience; I was separated from it by footlights that forced me into a proud exile which quickly turned to anguish.

Worst of all, I suspected the adults of faking. The words they spoke to me were candies, but they talked among themselves in quite another tone. And in addition, they sometimes broke sacred contracts. I would make my most adorable pout, the one about which I felt surest, and I would be told in a real voice: "Go play elsewhere, darling. We're talking." At other times, I felt that I was being used. My mother would take me to the Luxembourg. Uncle Emile, who was on the outs with the whole family, would suddenly turn up. He would look at his sister gloomily and say to her curtly: "It's not for your sake that I'm here. It's to see the child." He would then explain that I was the only innocent one in the family, the only one who had not deliberately offended him or condemned him to false relationships. I would smile, disturbed by my power and by the love I had kindled in the heart of that grim man. But the brother and sister were already discussing their affairs, listing their mutual grievances. Emile would rage against Charles; Anne Marie would defend him, though yielding ground; then they would go on to Louise. I would remain between their chairs, forgotten. I was prepared to grant—if only I had been old enough to understand them—all the reactionary maxims that an old liberal taught me by his behavior: that Truth and Fable are one and the same, that one must feign passion in order to feel it, that human life is a ceremony. I had been convinced that we were created for the purpose of laughing at the act we put on for each other. I accepted the act, but I required that I be the main character. But when lightning struck and left me blasted, I realized that I had a "false major role," that though I had lines to speak and was often on stage, I had no scene "of my own," in short, that I was giving the grown-ups their cues. Charles made much of me in order to cajole his death; Louise found in my liveliness a justification for her sulkiness, as Anne Marie did for her humility. Nevertheless, even without me, my mother would have been taken back by her parents, and her delicacy would have left her defenseless against Mamie; even without me, Louise would have sulked and Charles would have marveled at the Matterhorn, at meteors, or at the children of others. I was the opportunity that occasioned their quarrels and reconciliations; the deeper causes were elsewhere, in Mâcon, in Gunsbach, in an old, grimy yard, in a past long before my birth. I reflected back to them the unity of the family and its ancient conflicts; they were using my divine childhood to become what they were. I lived in a state of uneasiness: at the very moment when their ceremonies convinced me that nothing exists without a reason and that everyone, from the highest to the lowest, has his place marked out for him in the universe, my own reason for being slipped away; I would suddenly discover that I did not really count, and I felt ashamed of my unwonted presence in that well ordered world.

A father would have weighted me with a certain stable obstinacy. Making his moods my principles, his ignorance my knowledge, his disappointments my pride, his quirks my law, he would have inhabited me. That respectable tenant would have given me self-respect, and on that respect I would have based my right to live. My begetter would have determined my future. As a born graduate of the Ecole Polytechnique, I would have felt reassured forever. But if Jean-Baptiste Sartre had ever known my destination, he had taken the secret with him. My mother remembered only his saying: "My son won't go into the Navy." For want of more precise information, nobody, beginning with me, knew why the hell I had been born. Had he left me property, my childhood would have been changed. I would not be writing, since I would be someone else. House and field reflect back to the young heir a stable image of himself. He touches himself on *his* gravel, on the diamond-shaped panes of *his* veranda, and makes of their inertia the deathless substance of his soul. A few days ago, in a restaurant, the owner's son, a little seven-year-old, cried out to the cashier: "When my father's not here, *I'm* the boss!" There's a man for you! At his age, I was nobody's master and nothing belonged to me. In my rare moments of lavishness, my mother would whisper to me: "Be careful! We're not in our own home!" We were never in our own home, neither on the Rue le Goff nor later, when my mother remarried. This caused me no suffering since everything was loaned to me, but I remained abstract. Worldly possessions reflect to their owner what he is; they taught me what I was not. *I was not* substantial or permanent, *I was not* the future continuer of my father's work, *I was not* necessary to the production of steel. In short, I had no soul.

Things would have been fine if my body and I had got on well together. But the fact is that we were an odd couple. When a child is unhappy, he doesn't ask himself questions. If he suffers *bodily* as a result of needs and sickness, his unjustifiable state justifies his existence. His right to live is based on hunger, on the constant danger of death. He lives in order not to die. As for me, I was neither rich enough to think I was predestined nor poor enough to feel my desires as demands. I performed my alimentary duties, and God sometimes—rarely—blessed me with the grace that enables one to eat without disgust, namely appetite. Breathing, digesting, defecat-

ing unconcernedly, I lived because I had begun
to live. I was unaware of the violence and savage
demands of that gorged companion, my body,
which made itself known by a series of mild disturbances, much in demand among grown-ups.
At the time, a self-respecting family was in duty
bound to have at least one delicate child. I was
exactly what was needed, since I had almost died
at birth. The family kept its eye on me; they felt
my pulse, took my temperature, made me stick
out my tongue: "Don't you think he's a bit pale?"
"It's the light." "I assure you, he's lost weight!"
"But Papa, we weighed him yesterday." Beneath
those inquiring gazes I felt myself becoming an
object, a flower in a pot. I would finally be put
to bed. Suffocating with heat, simmering under
the sheets, I lumped my body with its discomfort:
I did not know which of the two was undesirable.

M. Simonnot, my grandfather's associate,
lunched with us on Thursdays. I envied that
middle-aged gentleman with girlish cheeks who
waxed his moustache and dyed his toupet. When
Anne Marie asked him, to keep the conversation
going, whether he liked Bach, whether he enjoyed
the seashore or the mountains, whether he had
pleasant memories of his native town, he would
take time to reflect and would direct his inner
gaze to the granite-like mass of his tastes. When
he had obtained the information that had been

requested, he would communicate it to my mother in an objective tone accompanied by a nod of his head. Lucky man! He no doubt awoke every morning in a jubilant state, glanced at his peaks, crests, and vales, then stretched voluptuously, saying to himself: "Yes, it's I. I'm M. Simonnot all over." Of course, I was quite able, when questioned, to state my preferences and even assert them. But when I was alone, they eluded me. Far from feeling them, I had to hold on to them and push them, to breathe life into them. I was no longer even sure that I preferred beef tenderloin to roast veal. What would I not have given to be the seat of a contorted landscape, of an obstinacy and persistency upright as a cliff. When Mme. Picard, using the vocabulary that was fashionable at the time, said of my grandfather: "Charles is an exquisite being," or: "There's no knowing human beings," I felt condemned beyond appeal. The pebbles in the Luxembourg, M. Simonnot, Karlémami, those were human beings. Not I. I had neither their inertia, their depth nor their impenetrability. I was *nothing*: an ineffaceable transparency. My jealousy knew no bounds the day I learned that M. Simonnot, that statue, that monolithic block, was, in addition, indispensable to the universe.

There was a party. At the Modern Language Institute, the crowd clapped hands beneath the

shifting flame of an incandescent burner, my
mother played Chopin, everyone spoke French
with faded graces and the pomp of an oratorio.
I flew from one to the other without touching
the ground; I was being stifled against the breast
of a German lady-novelist when my grandfather,
from the height of his glory, issued a verdict that
stabbed my heart: "There's someone missing
here: Simonnot." I escaped from the lady-novelist's arms, I took refuge in a corner. In the cen-
ter of a tumultuous ring, I saw a column: M.
Simonnot himself, absent in the flesh. That prodigious absence transfigured him. The attendance
was far from complete: certain pupils were sick,
others had asked to be excused, but these were
merely accidental and negligible facts. M. Simonnot alone was *missing*. The mere mention
of his name had sufficed for emptiness to sink
like a knife into the crowded room. It astounded
me that a man had his place marked out for him.
His place: a nothingness hollowed out by universal expectation, an invisible womb from which,
so it seemed, one could suddenly be reborn. Yet
if he had sprung up from the floor amidst an
ovation, even if the women had rushed to kiss
his hand, I would have calmed down: bodily
presence is always a surplus. But intact, reduced
to the purity of a negative essence, he retained
the incompressible transparency of a diamond.
Since it was my personal lot to be situated, every

single moment, among certain persons, in a certain place on earth, and to know that I was superfluous there, I wanted to be missed, like water, like bread, like air, by all other men in all other places.

That wish rose to my lips every day. Charles Schweitzer saw necessity everywhere in order to cover up an anguish that was never apparent to me when he was alive and that I begin to sense only now. All his colleagues held up the sky. Those Atlases included grammarians, philologists and linguists, M. Lyon-Caen, and the editor of the *Pedagogic Review*. He spoke of them sententiously so that we would realize their full importance: "Lyon-Caen knows his business. His place is at the Institute," or "Shurer is getting old. Let's hope they won't be so foolish as to pension him off. The Faculty doesn't realize what it would be losing." Surrounded by irreplaceable old men whose approaching demise was going to plunge Europe into mourning and perhaps the world into barbarism, what would I not have given to hear a fabulous voice proclaim solemnly in my heart: "That little Sartre knows his business. France doesn't realize what she'd be losing if he passed away." A bourgeois child lives in the eternity of the instant, that is, in a state of inaction. I wanted to be an Atlas right away, forever, and since the beginning of time. It did not even occur to me that one could work to become one. I needed a Supreme Court, a decree restoring my rights to me. But where were the magistrates? My natural judges had fallen into discredit through their hamming; I objected to them, but I saw no others.

A bewildered vermin, a waif and stray, without reason or purpose, I escaped into the family play-acting, twisting and turning, running, flying from imposture to imposture. I fled from my unjustifiable body and its dreary confidences. If the spinning top collided with an obstacle and stopped, the frenzied little ham would relapse into an animal stupor. Good friends said to my mother that I was sad, that they had seen me dreaming. My mother hugged me to her, with a laugh: "You who are so gay, always singing! What could you possibly complain about? You have everything you want." She was right. A spoiled child isn't sad; he's bored, like a king. Like a dog.

I'm a dog. I yawn, the tears roll down my cheeks, I feel them. I'm a tree, the wind gets caught in my branches and shakes them vaguely. I'm a fly, I climb up a windowpane, I fall, I start climbing again. Now and then, I feel the caress of time as it goes by. At other times—most often—I feel it standing still. Trembling minutes drop down, engulf me, and are a long time dying. Wallowing, but still alive, they're swept away. They are replaced by others which are fresher but equally futile. This disgust is called happiness. My mother keeps telling me that I'm the happiest of little boys. How could I not believe it *since it's true*? I never think about my forlornness. To begin with, there's no word for it. And secondly, I don't see it. I always have people around me. Their presence is the warp and woof of my life, the stuff of my pleasures, the flesh of my thoughts.

I saw death. When I was five, it lay in wait for me. In the evening, it would prowl on the balcony, press its nose against the window. I saw it, but I dared not say anything. Once we met it on the Quai Voltaire. It was an old lady, tall and mad, dressed in black. She muttered as I passed: "I'll put that child in my pocket." Another time, it assumed the form of an excavation. We were in Arcachon. Karlémami and my mother were visiting Mme. Dupont and her son Gabriel, the composer. I was playing in the garden of the cottage, frightened because I had been told that Gabriel was sick and was going to die. I played horse, half-heartedly, and capered around the house. Suddenly I saw a shadowy hole: the cellar had been opened. I do not quite know what manifestation of loneliness and hor-

ror blinded me; I turned around and, singing at
the top of my voice, ran away. In that period, I
had an appointment with it every night in bed.
This was a rite. I had to lie on my left side, with
my face to the wall. I would wait, all atremble,
and it would appear, a very run-of-the-mill skele-
ton with a scythe. I was then allowed to turn on
my right side. It would go away. I could sleep
in peace. During the day, I recognized it beneath
the most varied disguises: if my mother happened to sing the *Erlking* in French, I would
stop my ears. After reading *The Drunkard and
His Wife,* I went for six months without opening La Fontaine's fables. The fiend didn't give
a damn. Hidden in a story by Mérimée, *The
Venus of Ille,* it waited for me to read and
sprang at my throat. Funerals didn't bother me,
nor did graves. Around that time, my grandmother Sartre fell ill and died. My mother and
I, summoned by telegram, arrived in Thiviers
while she was still alive. The family thought it
advisable to send me away from the place where
that long, unhappy existence was coming to an
end. Friends took care of me and put me up. To
keep me busy, they gave me educational games
that reeked of boredom. I played, I read, I made
an earnest effort to display an exemplary state
of composure, but I felt nothing. Nor did I feel
anything when we followed the hearse to the
cemetery. Death shone by its absence: to pass

away was not to die. The metamorphosis of that
old woman into a tombstone did not displease
me. There was a transubstantiation, an accession
to being; in short, it was as if I had been transformed, pompously, into M. Simonnot. For that
reason, I have always liked, I still like, Italian
cemeteries: the stone is tormented there; it is a
whole baroque man; an encrusted medallion
frames a photo which recalls the deceased in his
first state. When I was seven years old, I met
real Death, the Grim Reaper, everywhere, but
it was never there. What was it? A person and a
threat. The person was mad. As for the threat, it
was this: shadowy mouths could open anywhere,
in broad daylight, in the brightest sun, and snap
me up. Things had a horrible underside. When
one lost one's reason, one saw it. To die was to
carry madness to an extreme and to sink into it.
I lived in a state of terror; it was a genuine neurosis. If I seek the reason for it, I find the following: as a spoiled child, a gift of providence,
my profound uselessness was all the more manifest to me in that the family rite constantly
seemed to me a trumped-up necessity. I felt
superfluous; therefore, I had to disappear. I was
an insipid blossoming constantly on the point of
being nipped in the bud. In other words, I was
condemned; the sentence could be applied at any
moment. Nevertheless, I rejected it with all my
might. Not that my existence was dear to me;

on the contrary, because I wasn't keen on it: the more absurd the life, the less bearable the death.

God would have managed things for me. I would have been a signed masterpiece. Assured of playing my part in the universal concert, I would have patiently waited for Him to reveal His purposes and my necessity. I reached out for religion, I longed for it, it was the remedy. Had it been denied me, I would have invented it myself. It was not denied me. Raised in the Catholic faith, I learned that the Almighty had made me for His glory. That was more than I dared dream. But later, I did not recognize in the fashionable God in whom I was taught to believe the one whom my soul was awaiting. I needed a Creator; I was given a Big Boss. The two were one and the same, but I didn't realize it. I was serving, without zeal, the Idol of the Pharisees, and the official doctrine put me off seeking my own faith. What luck! Confidence and sorrow made my soul a choice soil for sowing the seeds of heaven. Were it not for that mistake, I would now be a monk. But my family had been affected by the slow movement of dechristianization that started among the Voltairian upper bourgeoisie and took a century to spread to all levels of society. Without that general weakening of faith, Louise Guillemin, a Catholic young lady from the provinces, would have made a show of greater reluctance to marry a Lutheran. Of course, our whole family believed in God, as a matter of discretion. Seven or eight years after the Combes cabinet, declared disbelief had the violence and raucousness of passion. An atheist was a "character," a wildman whom one did not invite to dinner lest he "lash out," a fanatic encumbered with taboos who refused the right to kneel in church, to weep sweetly there, to give his daughters a religious wedding, who took it upon himself to prove the truth of his doctrine by the purity of his morals, who hounded himself and his happiness to the point of depriving himself of the means of dying comforted, a God-obsessed crank who saw His absence everywhere and who could not open his mouth without uttering His name, in short, a gentleman who had religious convictions. The believer had none. For two thousand years, Christian certainties had had time to prove their worth. They belonged to everyone. They were asked to shine in the gaze of a priest, in the semi-darkness of a church, and to light up men's souls, but nobody had any need to assume them himself. They were the common heritage. Good Society believed in God in order not to speak of Him. How tolerant religion seemed! How comfortable it was: the Christian could desert the Mass and let his children marry in Church, could smile at "all that holy stuff" and shed tears as he listened to the Wedding March from *Lohengrin*. He was

not obliged either to lead an exemplary life or to
die in a state of despair; he was not even obliged
to be cremated. In our circle, in my family, faith
was merely a high-sounding name for sweet
French freedom. I had been baptized, like so
many others, in order to preserve my independ-
ence; in denying me baptism, the family would
have feared that it was doing violence to my soul.
As a registered Catholic, I was free, I was
normal. "Later," they said, "he'll do as he likes."
It was deemed at the time that it was much harder
to gain faith than to lose it.

Charles Schweitzer was too much of an actor
not to need a Great Spectator, but he hardly
ever thought about God except in big moments.
As he was sure of finding Him in the hour of
his death, he kept Him out of his life. In private
life, out of loyalty to our lost provinces, to the
coarse gaiety of his anti-papist brothers, he never
missed an opportunity to ridicule Catholicism.
His table-talk resembled that of Luther. He was
tireless on the subject of Lourdes: Bernadette
had seen a "countrywoman changing her che-
mise"; a paralytic had been dipped into the foun-
tain, and when he was taken out, "he could see
with both eyes." He related the life of Saint
Labre, who was covered with lice, that of Saint
Marie Alacoque, who licked up the excrement
of sick persons with her tongue. Those tall

stories were useful to me. I was all the more in-
clined to rise above worldly goods in that I possessed none, and I would have had no difficulty
in finding my vocation in my comfortable destitution. Mysticism suits displaced persons and superfluous children. To push me into it, it would
have been enough to present the matter to me by
the other end; I was in danger of being a prey
to saintliness. My grandfather disgusted me
with it forever. I saw it through his eyes. That
cruel madness sickened me by the dullness of its
ecstasies, terrified me by its sadistic contempt for
the body. The eccentricities of the saints made no
more sense to me than those of Englishmen who
dived into the sea in evening clothes. When
listening to these stories, my grandmother pretended to be indignant. She called her husband
an "infidel" and a "heretic." She rapped him on
the knuckles, but the indulgence of her smile
finally opened my eyes. She believed in nothing.
Her scepticism alone kept her from being an
atheist. My mother was careful not to intervene.
She had "her own God" and asked him little more
than to comfort her in secret. The discussion
would continue in my head, in milder fashion.
Another me, my grim brother, would languidly
challenge all the articles of faith. I was a Catholic
and a Protestant; I united the critical spirit and
the spirit of submission. At bottom, the whole
business bored me. I was led to disbelief not by

the conflict of dogmas, but by my grandparents'
indifference. Nevertheless, I believed. In my
nightshirt, kneeling on the bed, with my hands
together, I said my prayers every day, but I
thought of God less and less often. On Thursdays, my mother took me to the Abbé Dibildos
Institute, where I was given religious instruction
amidst unknown children. My grandfather had
done such a thorough job that I regarded priests
as odd animals. Although they were ministers
of *my* persuasion, they were stranger to me than
Protestant pastors because of their robe and their
celibacy. Charles Schweitzer respected Abbé Dibildos—"an upright man!"—whom he knew per-
sonally, but his anti-clericalism was so outspoken
that I would go through the doorway with the
feeling of entering enemy territory. As for myself, I did not hate priests. When they spoke to
me, their faces took on a gentle expression, as if
they were being massaged with spirituality, a
look of wonderstruck kindliness, the infinite gaze
that I appreciated particularly in Mme. Picard
and other old musician friends of my mother. It
was my grandfather who hated them through
me. It was he who had first had the idea of committing me to the care of his friend the abbé, but
he would gaze anxiously at the little Catholic who
was brought back to him on Thursday afternoon.
He would seek in my eyes the progress of papery
and did not abstain from twitting me. This false

situation did not last more than six months. One day, I handed in to the teacher a French composition on the Passion. It had delighted my family, and my mother had recopied it with her own hand. It was awarded only the silver medal. This disappointment drove me into impiety. An illness and then vacation prevented me from returning to the Dibildos Institute. When school began, I insisted that I not go back at all. For several years more, I maintained public relations with the Almighty. But privately, I ceased to associate with Him. Only once did I have the feeling that He existed. I had been playing with matches and burned a small rug. I was in the process of covering up my crime when suddenly God saw me. I felt His gaze inside my head and on my hands. I whirled about in the bathroom, horribly visible, a live target. Indignation saved me. I flew into a rage against so crude an indiscretion, I blasphemed, I muttered like my grandfather: "God damn it, God damn it, God damn it." He never looked at me again.

I have just related the story of a missed vocation: I needed God, He was given to me, I received Him without realizing that I was seeking Him. Failing to take root in my heart, He vegetated in me for a while, then He died. Whenever anyone speaks to me about Him today, I say, with the easy amusement of an old beau who

meets a former belle: "Fifty years ago, had it
not been for that misunderstanding, that mistake,
the accident that separated us, there might have
been something between us."

There was nothing. Yet things were going
from bad to worse for me. My long hair got on
my grandfather's nerves. "He's a boy," he would
say. "You're going to make a girl of him. I don't
want my grandson to become a sissy!" Anne
Marie stuck to her guns. She would, I think, have
liked me to be a girl really and truly. That would
have revived her sad childhood, and she would
have been able to heap blessings on it. But since
Heaven had not heard her prayer, she made her
own arrangements: I would have the sex of the
angels, indeterminate, but feminine around the
edges. Being gentle, she taught me gentleness;
my solitude did the rest and kept me away from
violent games. One day—I was seven years old—
my grandfather could no longer stand it. He took
me by the hand, saying that we were going for
a walk. But no sooner had we got around the
corner than he rushed me into a barber shop,
saying: "We're going to give your mother a
surprise." I adored surprises. We were always
surprising each other at home. Amused or virtuous shows of mystery, unexpected gifts, theatrical revelations followed by hugs and kisses: that
was the tone of our life. When my appendix was

removed, my mother had not breathed a word about it to Karl so as to spare him the anguish which, in any case, he would not have felt. My uncle Auguste had given the money. We had secretly returned from Arcachon and had hidden in a clinic at Courbevoie. The day after the operation, Auguste had gone to see my grandfather: "I have good news for you," he said. Karl was taken in by the kindly serenity of his voice: "You're remarrying!" "No," replied my uncle with a smile, "but everything went off very well." "What everything?" Etc., etc. In short, dramatic happenings were part of my daily routine, and I good-humoredly watched my curls roll down the white sheet around my neck and fall to the floor, inexplicably tarnished. I returned home shorn and glorious.

There were shrieks, but no hugging and kissing, and my mother locked herself in her room to cry. Her little girl had been exchanged for a little boy. But that wasn't the worst of it. As long as my lovely ringlets fluttered about my ears, they made it possible to deny my obvious ugliness. Yet my right eye was already entering the twilight. She had to admit the truth to herself. My grandfather himself seemed nonplussed. He had been entrusted with her little wonder and had brought back a toad. The very foundations

of his future delights were being undermined.
Mamie looked at him in amusement. She simply
said: "Karl's not proud of what he's done. He
looks glum."

Anne Marie had the kindness to conceal from
me the cause of her grief. I didn't learn what it
was until I was twelve, and I was hit hard. But
I had a general feeling of uneasiness. I would
often catch friends of the family looking at me
with a worried or puzzled expression. My audience was getting more and more difficult. I had
to exert myself. I overplayed and sounded false.
I knew the anguish of an aging actress. I learned
that others could please too. Two striking memories remain with me, though they date from a
little later.

I was nine years old. It was raining. There
were ten children at the hotel in Noirétable, ten
cats in the same bag. To keep us busy, my grandfather decided to write and stage a patriotic
play with ten characters. Bernard, the oldest of
the group, played the role of Struthoff, a gruff
but kindly old fellow. I was a young Alsatian:
my father had chosen France, and I was sneaking across the border to join him. I had a number of bravura speeches: I would put out my
right arm, bow my head and murmur, hiding my

prelate-like cheek in the hollow of my shoulder: "Farewell, farewell, our dear Alsace." During rehearsals, the adults said I was just too sweet for words; that didn't surprise me. The performance took place in the garden. The stage was marked off by two clumps of shrubs and the wall of the hotel. The parents were sitting in cane chairs. The children were having a wonderful time; except me. Convinced that the fate of the play was in my hands, I made a particular effort to please, out of devotion to the common cause. I felt that all eyes were fixed on me. I overdid it; the applause went to Bernard, who was less affected. Did I realize it? At the end of the performance, he took up a collection. I slipped up behind him and tugged at his beard, which came away in my hand. It was a star's whim; just for the fun of it. I felt utterly charming and hopped from one foot to the other, brandishing my trophy. Nobody laughed. My mother took me by the hand and briskly led me aside: "Whatever got into you?" she asked, with a woebegone look. The beard was so nice! Everyone uttered an "Oh!" of astonishment. My grandmother immediately joined us with the latest news: Bernard's mother had spoken of jealousy. "You see what you get by showing off!" I escaped, ran to our room, planted myself in front of the mirror-wardrobe, and made faces for a long time.

Mme. Picard was of the opinion that a child can read everything: "A book never does any harm if it's well written." I had once asked permission, in her presence, to read *Madame Bovary,* and my mother had turned on her too musical voice: "But if my little darling reads books of that kind at his age, what will he do when he grows up?"—"I'll live them!" This reply had had a definite and permanent success. Every time Mme. Picard visited us, she alluded to it, and my mother would exclaim in a flattered tone: "Blanche! Do be quiet, you're going to spoil him!" I loved and despised that pale, fat old woman who was my best audience. When I was told she was coming, I felt I was a genius. I dreamed that she lost her skirts and that I saw her behind, which was a way of paying tribute to her spirituality. In November 1915, she presented me with a red leather, gilt-edged booklet. My grandfather was away, and we were sitting in the study. The women were talking animatedly, a tone lower than in 1914 because it was wartime. A dirty yellow haze clung to the windows; there was a stale smell of tobacco. I opened the notebook and was at first disappointed. I was hoping for a novel, a story book. Over and over I read the same questionnaire on the multicolored pages: "Fill it in and have your little friends do the same. You will be building happy memories." I decided to answer then and

there, sat down at my grandfather's desk, laid
the booklet on his blotter, took his plastic pen-
holder, dipped it into the bottle of red ink, and
began to write while the grown-ups exchanged
amused glances. With a single leap I had
perched higher than my soul in order to hunt for
"answers beyond my age." Unfortunately, the
questionnaire was not helpful. I was asked about
my likes and dislikes: what was my favorite
color, my favorite smell? I half-heartedly invented predilections. Suddenly there was an opportunity to shine: "What is your fondest wish?"
I replied without hesitation: "To be a soldier and
avenge the dead." Then, too excited to go on, I
jumped down and took my work over to the
grown-ups. Their expressions grew sharp. Mme.
Picard adjusted her glasses; my mother leaned
over her shoulder; both of them pursed their lips
quizzically. Their heads bobbed up together. My
mother had turned pink. Mme. Picard gave the
book back to me: "You know, my dear, it's in-
teresting only if you're sincere." I thought I
would die. My mistake was glaring: she had asked
for the child prodigy; I had given the sublime
child. Unfortunately for me, those ladies had nobody at the front. Military sublimity had no effect on their moderate souls. I disappeared and
went to make faces in front of a mirror. When I
think back to those faces, I realize that they were
a means of protection: I defended myself against

blazing bursts of shame by a tightening of muscles. In addition, by carrying my misfortune to an extreme, this reaction freed me from it: I rushed into humility in order to evade humiliation. I did away with the means of pleasing so as to forget that I had had them and had misused them. The mirror was of great help to me: I made it teach me that I was a monster. If it succeeded, my sharp remorse would change into pity. But, above all, as the failure had revealed my servility to me, I made myself hideous so as to make it impossible, so as to reject human beings, and so that they would reject me. The Comedy of Evil was being performed against the Comedy of Good; Eliakim was playing Quasimodo's role. By combined twists and puckers I was distorting my face; I was vitriolizing myself in order to efface my former smiles.

The remedy was worse than the disease: I had tried to take shelter against glory and dishonor in my lonely truth. But I had no truth. All I found in myself was an astonished insipidness. Before my eyes, a jelly-fish was hitting against the glass of the aquarium, wrinkling its flabby collaret, fraying in the darkness. Night fell, clouds of ink were diluted in the mirror, swallowing up my final embodiment. Deprived of an alibi, I fell upon myself. In the darkness, I sensed an indefinite hesitation, a faint touch, a throbbing, a whole living creature—the most terrifying and the only one of which I couldn't be afraid. I fled, I went back to resume, in the light, my role of soiled cherub. In vain. The mirror had taught me what I had always known: I was horribly natural. I have never got over that.

Idolized by all, rejected by each, I was left out of things, and my sole recourse, at the age of seven, was within myself, who did not yet exist, a glass palace in which the budding century beheld its boredom. I had been born in order to fill the great need I had of myself. Until then, I had known only the conceit of a lap-dog. Driven into pride, I became the Proud One. Since nobody laid claim to me *seriously,* I laid claim to being indispensable to the Universe. What could be haughtier? What could be sillier? The fact is that I had no choice. I had sneaked on to the train and had fallen asleep, and when the ticket-collector shook me and asked for my ticket, I had to admit that I had none. Nor did I have the money with which to pay my fare on the spot. I began by pleading guilty. I had left my identity card at home, I no longer even remembered how I had gotten by the ticket-puncher, but I admitted that I had sneaked on to the train. Far from challenging the authority of the ticket-collector, I loudly proclaimed my respect for his functions

and complied in advance with his decision. At
that extreme degree of humility, the only way I
could save myself was by reversing the situation:
I therefore revealed that I had to be in Dijon for
important and secret reasons, reasons that concerned France and perhaps all mankind. If things
were viewed in this new light, it would be apparent that no one in the entire train had as much
right as I to occupy a seat. Of course, this involved a higher law which conflicted with the
regulations, but if the ticket-collector took it
upon himself to interrupt my journey, he would
cause grave complications, the consequences of
which would be *his* responsibility. I urged him
to think it over: was it reasonable to doom the
entire species to disorder under the pretext of
maintaining order in a train? Such is pride: the
plea of the wretched. Only passengers with tickets have the right to be modest. I never knew
whether I won my case. The ticket-collector remained silent. I repeated my arguments. So long
as I spoke, I was sure he wouldn't make me get
off. We remained face to face, one mute and the
other inexhaustible, in the train that was taking
us to Dijon. The train, the ticket-collector, and
the delinquent were myself. And I was also a
fourth character, the organizer, who had only
one wish, to fool himself, if only for a minute,
to forget that he had concocted everything. The
family play-acting was useful to me: I was called

a gift from heaven; that was just in fun and I was aware of it; crammed with coddling, I had ready tears and a hard heart. I wanted to become a useful gift in quest of its recipients. I offered my person to France, to the world. I didn't care a damn about human beings, but since they were involved, their tears of joy would inform me that the universe welcomed me with gratitude. The reader may think I was very bumptious. No, I was a fatherless orphan. Being nobody's son, I was my own cause and was filled with both pride and wretchedness. I had been brought into the world by the momentum that impelled me toward Good. The tie-up seems clear: feminized by maternal tenderness, dulled by the absence of the stern Moses who had begotten me, puffed with pride by my grandfather's adoration, I was a pure object, doomed par excellence to masochism if only I could have believed in the family playacting. But no. It perturbed me only on the surface, and the depths remained cold, unjustified. The system horrified me. I developed a hatred of happy swoons, of abandonment, of that caressed and coddled body. I found myself by opposing myself. I plunged into pride and sadism, in other words, into generosity, which, like avarice or race prejudice, is only a secret balm for healing our inner wounds and which ends by poisoning us. In order to escape the forlornness of the creature, I was preparing for myself the most irremediable bourgeois solitude, that of the creator. This shift is not to be confused with genuine revolt: one rebels against an oppressor and I had only benefactors. I remained their accomplice for a long time. Besides, it was they who had dubbed me a "gift of Providence." I merely used the instruments at my disposal for other purposes.

Everything took place in my head. Imaginary child that I was, I defended myself with my imagination. When I examine my life from the age of six to nine, I am struck by the continuity of my spiritual exercises. Their content often changed, but the program remained unvaried. I had made a false entrance; I withdrew behind a screen and began my birth over again at the right moment, the very minute that the universe silently called for me.

My first stories were merely a repetition of The Blue Bird, of Puss in Boots, of the tales of Maurice Bouchor. They talked to themselves behind my forehead, between my eyebrows. Later, I dared touch them up, I gave myself a role in them. They changed nature. I didn't like fairies; there were too many of them around me. The magical element was replaced by feats of valor. I became a hero. I cast off my charms. It was no longer a matter of pleasing, but of impressing. I abandoned my family. Karlémami and Anne

Marie were excluded from my fantasies. Sated
with gestures and attitudes, I performed real acts
in my reveries. I invented a difficult and mortal
universe, that of Cri-Cri, of The Stunner, of
Paul d'Ivoi. Instead of work and need, about
which I knew nothing, I introduced danger.
Never was I further from challenging the established order. Assured of living in the best of
worlds, I made it my business to purge it of its
monsters. As cop and lyncher, I sacrificed a gang
of bandits every evening. I never engaged in a
preventive war or carried out punitive measures.
I killed without pleasure or anger, in order to
save young ladies from death. Those frail creatures were indispensable to me; they called out
for me. Obviously they could not have counted on
my help since they did not know me. But I thrust
them into such great perils that nobody could
have rescued them unless he were I. When the
janissaries brandished their curved scimitars, a
moan went through the desert and the rocks said
to the sand: "Someone's missing here. It's Sartre." At that very moment I pushed aside the
screen. I struck out with my sabre and sent heads
flying. I was being born in a river of blood. Oh,
blessed steel! I was where I belonged.

I was born in order to die: the child, saved,
threw herself into the arms of her father, the
margrave. I left the scene. I had to become un-

necessary again or seek out new murderers. I
found them. Champion of the established order,
I had placed the be-all and end-all of my life in
a perpetuated disorder. I crushed Evil in my
arms; I died with its death and was reborn with
its resuscitation; I was a right-wing anarchist.
None of this righteous violence was apparent. I
remained servile and zealous: the habit of virtue
is not so easily lost. But every evening I looked
forward impatiently to the end of the daily clowning. I would hurry to bed, reel off my prayers,
and slip between the sheets. I was eager to get
back to my mad recklessness. I grew older in the
darkness, I became a lonely adult, without father
and mother, without home or hearth, almost without a name. I would walk on a flaming roof, carrying in my arms an unconscious woman. The
crowd was screaming below me. It was obvious
to all that the building was going to collapse. At
that moment, I would utter the fateful words:
"Continued in the next installment."—"What
did you say?" my mother would ask. I would
answer cautiously: "I'm leaving myself in sus-
pense." And the fact is that I would fall asleep,
amidst those perils, in a state of thrilling inse-
curity. The next evening, faithful to my troth,
I was back on the roof, confronted with the flames,
with sure death. Suddenly I would spot a rain-
pipe which I hadn't noticed the night before. Oh
God, saved! But how could I hold on to it without

letting go of my precious burden? Fortunately
the young woman was coming back to her senses.
I put her on my back, she wrapped her arms
around my neck. No, on second thought, I thrust
her back into unconsciousness: however little
she contributed to my rescue, my merit would
have been reduced thereby. By chance, there was
that rope at my feet. I attached the victim firmly
to her rescuer. The rest was child's play. Distinguished gentlemen—the mayor, the chief of police, the fire chief—received me in their arms,
kissed my cheeks, gave me a medal. I lost my self-
assurance, I no longer knew what to do with
myself. The embraces of those dignitaries were
too much like those of my grandfather. I crossed
out everything. I began all over. It was night-
time, a young lady was calling for help, I threw
myself into the fray . . . *Continued in the next
installment.* I risked my neck for the sublime
moment that would change a chance creature into
a providential passer-by, but I felt I would not
survive my victory and was only too happy to
put it off until the following day.

It may surprise the reader to find these dare-
devil dreams in a scribbler destined to an intellectual career. The anxieties of childhood are metaphysical. There is no need to shed blood in order
to calm them. Did I therefore never want to be
a heroic doctor and save my fellow-countrymen

from the bubonic plague or cholera? Never, I admit it. Yet I was neither ferocious nor warlike, and it is no fault of mine if the budding century gave me an epic cast of mind. France, which had been beaten, swarmed with imaginary heroes whose exploits soothed her self-esteem. Eight years before my birth, Cyrano de Bergerac had "burst like a fanfare of red trousers." A little later, L'Aiglon, proud and ravaged, had only to appear to wipe away the Fachoda incident. In 1912, I knew nothing about those lofty characters, but I was in constant touch with their epigones. I adored the Cyrano of the Underworld, Arsène Lupin, without knowing that he owed his herculean strength, his courage and his very French intelligence to the drubbing we had taken in 1870. The national aggressiveness and spirit of revenge made all children avengers. I became an avenger like everyone else. Charmed by French banter and dash, those intolerable blemishes of the vanquished, I twitted my villains before knocking them out. But wars bored me. I was fond of the quiet Germans who visited my grandfather, and I was interested only in private injustices. Collective forces were transformed in my unhating heart; I used them to feed my individual heroism. Be that as it may, I am a marked man. If I have committed the mad blunder, in a grim century, of taking life for an epic, it is because I am a grandchild of the defeat. Convinced materialist that I am, my epic idealism will compensate, until I die, for an affront and a shame which I never suffered, for the loss of two provinces which we got back a long time ago.

The bourgeois of the last century never forgot their first evening at the theatre, and their writers undertook to tell what it was like. When the curtain went up, children thought they were at court. The gold and crimson, the lights, the make-up, the bombast and artifice, introduced the element of the sacred even into crime. The nobility that their grandfathers had murdered came to life again on the stage. During intermission, the division into balconies presented them with an image of society. They were shown bare shoulders and live nobles in the boxes. They returned home dumbfounded, softened up, insidiously prepared for ceremonious destinies, prepared to become Jules Favre, Jules Ferry, Jules Grévy. I defy my contemporaries to tell me the date of the first movie they saw. We blindly entered a century without traditions, a century that was to contrast strongly with the others by its bad manners, and the new art, the art of the common man, foreshadowed our barbarism. Born in a den of thieves, officially classified as a traveling show, it had popular ways that shocked serious people. It was an amusement for women and children. My mother and I loved it, but we hardly gave it a thought and we never talked about it. Does one talk about bread if one has it? When we came to realize its existence, it had long since become our chief need.

On rainy days, Anne Marie would ask me what I felt like doing. We would hesitate for a long time between the circus, the Châtelet, the Electric House, and the Grévin Museum. At the last moment, with calculated casualness, we would decide to go to the movies. Once, as we were about to leave, my grandfather appeared at the door of his study and asked: "Where are you going, children?"—"To the movies," my mother answered. He frowned and she quickly added, "To the Panthéon Cinema. It's nearby. We just have to cross the Rue Soufflot." He let us leave, shrugging his shoulders. The following Thursday, he said to M. Simonnot: "Look here, Simonnot, you who are a serious man, do you understand it? My daughter takes my grandson to the cinema!" And M. Simonnot replied, in a conciliatory tone: "I've never been, but my wife sometimes goes."

The show had begun. We would stumblingly follow the usherette. I would feel I was doing something clandestine. Above our heads, a shaft of light crossed the hall; one could see dust and vapor dancing in it. A piano whinnied away.

Violet pears shone on the walls. The varnish-like smell of a disinfectant would bring a lump to my throat. The smell and the fruit of that living darkness blended within me: I ate the lamps of the emergency exit, I filled up on their acid taste. I would scrape my back against knees and take my place on a creaky seat. My mother would slide a folded blanket under my behind to raise me. Finally, I would look at the screen. I would see a fluorescent chalk and blinking landscapes streaked with showers; it always rained, even when the sun shone brightly, even in apartments. At times, an asteroid in flames would shoot across the drawing-room of a baroness without her seeming to be surprised. I liked that rain, that restless anxiety which played on the wall. The pianist would attack the overture to *Fingal's Cave* and everyone understood that the criminal was about to appear: the baroness would be frightened out of her wits. But her beautiful, sooty face would make way for a purple show-card: "End of Part I." The lights would go on, it was a sudden awakening. Where was I? In a school? In an official building? Not the slightest ornament: rows of flap-seats beneath which could be seen their springs, walls smeared with ochre, a floor strewn with cigarette stubs and gobs of spit. Confused murmurs filled the hall, language was reinvented, the usherette would walk up and down selling hard candies. My mother would buy me some,

I would put them into my mouth, I would suck the emergency lamps. The people would rub their eyes, everyone discovered his neighbors. Soldiers, maids from the neighborhood; a bony old man would be chewing tobacco; bare-headed working girls would laugh loudly. That world wasn't ours. Fortunately, here and there on that sea of heads were big fluttering hats which were reassuring.

The social hierachy of the theatre had given my grandfather and late father, who were accustomed to second balconies, a taste for ceremonial. When many people are together, they must be separated by rites; otherwise, they slaughter each other. The movies proved the opposite. This mingled audience seemed united by a catastrophe rather than a festivity. Etiquette, now dead, revealed the true bond among men: adhesion. I developed a dislike for ceremonies, I loved crowds. I have seen crowds of all kinds, but the only other time I have witnessed that nakedness, that sense of everyone's direct relationship to everyone else, that waking dream, that dim consciousness of the danger of being a man, was in 1940, in Stalag XII D.

My mother grew bolder, to the point of taking me to the boulevard houses: the Kinérama, the Folies Dramatiques, the Vaudeville, the Gaumont Palace, which was then called the Hippodrome. I saw *Zigomar* and *Fantômas, The Exploits of Maciste, The Mysteries of New York*. The gilding spoiled my pleasure. The Vaudeville, a former legitimate theatre, was unwilling to give up its former grandeur: until the very last minute, the screen was hidden by a red tassled curtain; three raps were given to announce the beginning of the performance; the orchestra would play an overture; the curtain would go up; the lights would go down. I was irritated by that incongruous ceremonial, by that dusty pomp, the only result of which was to move the characters further away. In the balcony, in the gallery, our fathers, impressed by the chandelier and the paintings on the ceiling, neither could nor would believe that the theatre belonged to them: they were received there. As for me, I wanted to see the film *as close up as possible*. I had learned in the equalitarian discomfort of the neighborhood houses that this new art was mine, just as it was everyone else's. We had the same mental age: I was seven and knew how to read; it was twelve and did not know how to talk. People said that it was in its early stages, that it had progress to make; I thought that we would grow up together. I have not forgotten our common childhood: whenever I am offered a hard candy, whenever a woman varnishes her nails near me, whenever I inhale a certain smell of disinfectant in the toilet of a provincial hotel, whenever I see the violet bulb on the ceiling of a night-train, my eyes, nostrils, and tongue recapture the lights and odors of those bygone halls; four years ago, in rough weather off the coast of Fingal's Cave, I heard a piano in the wind.

Though impervious to the sacred, I loved magic. The cinema was a suspect appearance that I loved perversely for what it still lacked. That streaming was everything, it was nothing, it was everything reduced to nothing. I was witnessing the delirium of a wall; solids had been freed from a massiveness that weighed on me, that weighed even on my body, and my young idealism was delighted with that infinite contraction. At a later time, the transpositions and rotations of triangles reminded me of the gliding figures on the screen. I loved the cinema even in plane geometry. To me, black and white were the super-colors that contained all the others and revealed them only to the initiate; I was thrilled at seeing the invisible. Above all, I liked the incurable muteness of my heroes. But no, they weren't mute, since they knew how to make themselves understood. We communicated by means of music; it was the sound of their inner life. Persecuted innocence did better than merely show or speak of suffering: it permeated me with its pain by means of the melody that issued from it. I would read the conversations, but I heard the hope and bitterness; I would perceive by ear the proud grief that remains silent. I was compromised; the young widow who wept on the screen *was not I*, and yet she and I had only one soul: Chopin's funeral march; no more was needed for her tears to wet my eyes. I felt I was a prophet without being able to foresee anything: even before the traitor betrayed, his crime entered me; when all seemed peaceful in the castle, sinister chords exposed the murderer's presence. How happy were those cowboys, those musketeers, those detectives: their future was there, in that premonitory music, and governed the present. An unbroken song blended with their lives, led them on to victory or death by moving toward its own end. They were expected: by the girl in danger, by the general, by the traitor lurking in the forest, by the friend who was tied up near a powder-keg and who sadly watched the flame run along the fuse. The course of that flame, the virgin's desperate struggle against her abductor, the hero's gallop across the plain, the interlacing of all those images, of all those speeds, and, beneath it all, the demonic movement of the "Race to the Abyss," an orchestral selection taken from *The Damnation of Faust* and adapted for the piano, all of this was one and the same: it was Destiny. The hero dismounted, put out the fuse, the traitor sprang at him, a duel with knives began: but the accidents of the duel likewise partook of the rigor of the musical development; they were fake accidents which ill concealed the universal order. What joy when the last knife stroke coincided with the last chord! I was utterly content, I had found the world in which I wanted to live, I touched the absolute. What an uneasy feeling when the lights went on: I had been wracked with love for the characters and they had disappeared, carrying their world with them. I had felt their victory in my bones; yet it was theirs and not mine. In the street I found myself superfluous.

I decided to lose the power of speech and to live in music. I had an opportunity to do this every afternoon around five o'clock. My grandfather was teaching his classes at the Modern Language Institute; my grandmother had retired to her room and was reading Gyp; my mother had given me my afternoon snack; she had got dinner under way and given final instructions to the maid; she would sit down at the piano and play Chopin's ballades, a Schumann sonata, Franck's symphonic variations, sometimes, at my request, the overture to *Fingal's Cave*. I would slip into the study; it was already dark there; two candles were burning on the piano. The semi-darkness served my purpose. I would seize my grandfather's ruler; it was my rapier; his paper-cutter was my dagger; I became then and there the flat image of a musketeer. Sometimes I had to wait for inspiration: to gain time, I the illustrious swashbuckler would decide that an important matter obliged me to remain incognito. I had to receive blows without hitting back and to display my courage by feigning cowardice. I would walk around the room, my eyes glowering, my head bowed, shuffling my feet. I would indicate by a sudden start from time to time that I had been slapped or kicked in the behind, but I was careful not to react; I made a mental note of my insulter's name. Finally, the music, of which I had taken a huge dose, began to act. The piano forced its rhythm on me like a voodoo drum. The Fantasia Impromptu substituted for my soul; it inhabited me, gave me an unknown past, a blazing and mortal future. I was possessed, the demon had seized me and was shaking me like a plum tree. To horse! I was mare and rider, bestrider and bestridden. I dashed over hill and dale, from the door to the window. "You're making too much noise. The neighbors will complain," my mother would say, without ceasing to play. I did not answer, since I was mute. I spy the duke, I dismount, I inform him by silent movements of my lips that I consider him illegitimate. He unleashes his henchmen. My whirling sword is a bulwark of steel. From time to time, I run someone through. Immediately I about-face, I become the stabbed ruffian,

I fall, I die on the carpet. Then I secretly withdraw from the corpse, I stand up again, I go back to my role of knight-errant. I played all the characters: as knight, I slapped the duke; I spun about; as duke, I received the slap. But I did not embody the wicked for long, because I was always impatient to return to the major role, to myself. Invincible, I triumphed over all. But, as in my nocturnal narratives, I put off my triumph indefinitely because I was afraid of the depression that would follow.

I'm defending a young countess against the King's own brother. What a slaughter! But my mother has turned the page; the allegro gives way to a tender adagio; I finish off the carnage in quick time, I smile at the lady. She loves me; the music says so. And I love her too, perhaps. My heart slowly fills with love. What does one do when one is in love? I take her arm, we stroll in the meadow. There must be more to it than that. Summoned in haste, the bandits and the duke's men help me out. They attack us, a hundred against one. I kill ninety of them, the other ten kidnap the countess.

This is the moment to look into my dismal years. The woman who loves me is held captive. The whole police force of the kingdom is after me. I'm an outlaw who's being hunted down, a poor unhappy wretch. All I have left is my conscience and my sword. I would pace the study with a woe-begone look. Chopin's passionate sadness would gradually fill me. Sometimes I would skim through my life, I would skip two or three years to assure myself that all would end well, that the King would restore my titles, my lands, and a fiancée almost intact and that he would ask my forgiveness. But I would immediately jump back to my unhappy situation of two or three years earlier. That moment charmed me; fiction merged with truth. As a heartsore vagabond seeking justice, I resembled, like a twin brother, the child who was at loose ends, a burden to him-self, in search of a reason for living, who prowled about, to a musical accompaniment, in his grand-father's study. Without dropping the role, I took advantage of the resemblance to amalgamate our destinies; reassured as to the final victory, I would regard my tribulations as the surest way to achieve it. I would see through my abjection to the future glory that was its true cause. Schu-mann's sonata would finally convince me: I was both the creature who despairs and the God who has always saved him since the beginning of time. What a joy to be able to be bursting with afflic-tion; I had a right to be on the outs with the universe. Weary of easy successes, I relished the delights of melancholy, the pungent pleasure of resentment. An object of the tenderest care, petted and coddled, without desires, I rushed headlong into an imaginary destitution. Eight years of felicity had ended only in giving me a taste for martyrdom. Instead of my usual judges, who were all predisposed in my favor, I set up a surly court that was ready to condemn me without a hearing. I wrested an acquittal from it, congratulations, a just retribution. I had read the story of Griselda a dozen times with a thrill of pleasure. Yet I did not like to suffer, and my early desires were cruel: the defender of so many princesses had no scruples about mentally spanking the little girl next door. What pleased me about that not very praiseworthy story was the victim's sadism and the inflexible virtue that ended with the fiendish husband on his knees. That was what I wanted for myself: to force the magistrates to kneel, to make them revere me so as to punish them for their bias. But I kept putting off the acquittal to the following day. I remained a future hero and longed for a consecration which I continually postponed.

I think that this double melancholy, which I actually felt and at which I played, was an expression of my disappointment. All my exploits, laid end to end, were only a string of random events. When my mother struck the final chords of the Fantasia Impromptu, I fell back into the memoryless time of fatherless orphans, of orphan-

less knights-errant. Whether as hero or school-
boy, doing the same dictations, the same doughty
deeds, over and over, I remained locked up in the
prison of repetition. Yet the future existed, the
movies had revealed it to me; I dreamed of having
a destiny. I finally got tired of Griselda's moping.
Though I kept postponing indefinitely the his-
toric minute of my glorification, I was not making an actual future of it. It was only a deferred
present.

It was about that time—1912 or 1913—that I
read *Michael Strogoff*. I wept with joy. What
a model life! The officer did not have to await
the convenience of bandits in order to show his
valor. A command from above had drawn him
from the background. He lived in order to obey
it, and he died of his triumph, for that glory was
a death. When the last page of the book had been
turned, Michael buried himself alive in his little
gilt-edged coffin. Not a single anxiety: he was
justified as soon as he made his first appearance.
Nor the slightest accident: it's true that he was
continually moving about, but important interests, his courage, the enemy's vigilance, the nature of the setting, the means of communication,
and a dozen other factors, all of them given in
advance, made it possible to show his position
on the map at every moment. No repetitions:
everything kept changing, he too had to change

constantly, his future showed him the way, he was guided by a star. Three months later, I re-read the novel with the same rapture. But I didn't like Michael; I found him too goody-goody. It was his destiny that I envied him. I worshipped in him the disguised Christian that I had been prevented from being. The Czar of all the Russias was God the Father. Raised up from nothingness by a special decree, Michael, who, like all creatures, was charged with one major mission, made his way through our vale of tears, brushing aside temptations and surmounting obstacles; he tasted of martyrdom, enjoyed supernatural assistance,* glorified his Creator, then, having accomplished his task, entered immortality. For me, that book was poison: was it true that certain individuals were chosen? Was their path laid out for them by the highest necessities? Saintliness repelled me; in Michael Strogoff it fascinated me because it had donned the trappings of heroism.

Nevertheless, I made no change in my pantomimes, and the idea of a mission remained up in the air. It was a bodiless ghost that never took shape and that I was unable to get rid of. Of course my allies, the kings of France, were at my beck and call and awaited only a sign to give me their orders. I did not ask for them. If one risks one's life out of obedience, what becomes of gen-

* Saved by the miracle of a tear.

erosity? Marcel Dunot, the iron-fisted boxer, surprised me every week by graciously doing more than his duty. Michael Strogoff, blind and covered with glorious wounds, could barely say that he had done his. I admired his valor, I disapproved of his humility. That courageous man had only the sky above his head; why did he bow it before the czar when it was for the czar to kiss his feet? But unless he demeaned himself, where could he find a mandate to live? This contradiction greatly troubled me. I tried at times to get around the difficulty: I, an unknown child, would hear of a dangerous mission; I threw myself at the king's feet, I begged him to entrust me with it. He refused. I was too young, the matter was too serious. I stood up. I challenged all his captains to a duel and promptly defeated them. The sovereign admitted he had been wrong: "Go then, since you so wish!" But I was not taken in by my stratagem, and I was quite aware that I had imposed myself. And besides, all those scarecrows disgusted me. I was a republican and a regicide. My grandfather had warned me against tyrants, whether they were called Louis XVI or Badinguet. Furthermore, every day I read the installment of Michel Zévaco's serial in *Le Matin*. That author of genius had invented, under the influence of Hugo, the republican cloak-and-dagger novel. His heroes represented the people; they made and unmade empires and predicted, in the fourteenth century, the French Revolution. Out of pure kindheartedness, they protected child kings and mad kings against their ministers and slapped wicked kings in the face. The greatest of them all, Pardaillan, was my master. Firmly planted on my spindly legs, I slapped Henry III and Louis XIII dozens of times in imitation of him. Was I going to place myself under their orders after that? In short, I could neither produce from myself the imperative mandate that would have justified my presence on this earth, nor recognize anyone else's right to issue it to me. I went back to my long rides, listlessly. I moped amidst the fray. A wool-gathering slaughterer, an apathetic martyr, I remained Griselda, for want of a czar, of a God, or quite simply of a father.

I led two lives, both of them untrue. Publicly, I was an impostor: the famous grandson of the celebrated Charles Schweitzer; alone, I sank into imaginary moping. I corrected my false glory by a false incognito. I had no trouble shifting from one role to the other; just as I was about to make my secret thrust, the key would turn in the lock, my mother's hands would suddenly be paralyzed and rest motionless on the piano, I would put the ruler back in the study and rush into my grandfather's arms. I would pull up his chair, bring him his fur-lined slippers, and question him about his day, referring to his pupils by name. However deep my dream might have been, I was never in danger of getting lost in it. Yet I was in a bad way: my truth threatened to remain, to the very end, the alternation of my lies.

There was another truth. Children played in the Luxembourg Gardens. I would draw near them. They would brush against me without seeing me. I would watch them with the eyes of a beggar. How strong and quick they were! How good-looking! In the presence of those flesh-and-blood heroes, I would lose my prodigious intelligence, my universal knowledge, my athletic physique, my blustering shrewdness. I would lean against a tree, waiting. At a blunt order from the leader of the band: "Step forth, Pardaillan, you'll be the prisoner," I would have given up all my privileges. Even a silent role would have made me happy. I would have been only too willing to be a wounded victim on a stretcher, a dead soldier. I was not given the opportunity. I had met my true judges, my contemporaries, my peers, and their indifference condemned me. I could not get over discovering myself through them: neither a wonder nor a jelly-fish. Just a little shrimp in whom no one was interested. My mother had difficulty hiding her indignation. That tall, handsome woman was not

at all troubled about my shortness. She regarded
it as perfectly natural. The Schweitzers were tall
and the Sartres short. I took after my father.
That was all there was to it. She rather liked
my being portable, at the age of eight, and easy
to handle. To her my small format was a pro-
longed infancy. But seeing that no one invited me
to play, her mother-love made her realize that I
was in danger of taking myself for a dwarf—
which I am not quite—and of suffering thereby.
To save me from despair, she would feign impatience: "What are you waiting for, you big silly?
Ask them whether they want to play with you."
I would shake my head. I would have accepted
the lowliest jobs, but it was a matter of pride not
to ask for them. She would point to the ladies
sitting in iron chairs and knitting: "Do you want
me to speak to their mothers?" I would beg her
to do nothing of the kind. She would take my
hand, we would leave, we would go from tree to
tree and from group to group, always entreating,
always excluded. At twilight, I would be back
on my perch, on the heights where the spirit blew,
where my dreams dwelt. I would avenge my mor-
tifications by a half dozen childish remarks and
by massacring a hundred henchmen. In any case,
things weren't going right.

I was saved by my grandfather. He drove me,
without meaning to, into a new imposture that
changed my life.

Part 2 WRITING

Charles Schweitzer had never taken himself for a writer, but the French language still filled him with wonder at the age of seventy because he had had a hard time learning it and it did not quite belong to him. He played with it, took pleasure in the words, loved to pronounce them, and his relentless diction did not spare a single syllable. When he had time, his pen would arrange them in bouquets. He was only too ready to shed luster on family and academic events by works written for the occasion: New Year wishes, birthday greetings, congratulations for wedding parties, speeches in verse for Saint Charlemagne's day, sketches, charades, verses in set rhymes, amiable

trivialities; at conventions, he improvised qua-
trains in German and French.

At the beginning of the summer, the two
women and I would leave for Arcachon before
my grandfather finished his courses. He would
write to us three times a week, two pages for
Louise, a post-script for Anne Marie and a whole
letter in verse for me. In order to make me fully
aware of my good fortune, my mother learned
and taught me the rules of prosody. Someone
taught me to scribble out a versified reply. I was
urged to finish it, I was helped. When the two
women sent off the letter, they laughed till the
tears came at the thought of the recipient's astonishment. I received by return mail a poem to
my glory; I replied with a poem. The habit was
formed; the grandfather and his grandson were
united by a new bond. They spoke to each other,
like the Indians, like the Montmartre pimps,
in a language from which women were barred.
I was given a rhyming dictionary. I became
a versifier. I wrote madrigals for Vévé, a
blond little girl who never left her couch and
who died a few years later. The little girl
didn't care a damn about them: she was an
angel. But the admiration of a large public
consoled me for this indifference. I have dug up a
few of these poems. All children have genius,
except Minou Drouet, said Cocteau in 1955. In

1912, they all had it, except me. I wrote in imitation, for the sake of the ceremony, in order to act like a grown-up; above all, I wrote because I was Charles Schweitzer's grandson. I was given La Fontaine's *Fables*. I didn't care for them: the author was too casual. I decided to rewrite them in alexandrines. The undertaking was too much for me, and I had an impression that it made the others smile. That was my last poetical experience. But I had got a start. I shifted from verse to prose and had not the slightest difficulty reinventing, in writing, the exciting adventures that I read in *Cri-Cri*. It was high time: I was going to discover the inanity of my dreams. In the course of my fantastic gallops, it was reality that I was seeking. When my mother would ask me, without taking her eyes from her score: "Poulou, what are you doing?", I would sometimes break my vow of silence and answer: "I'm playing moving-pictures." Indeed, I was trying to pluck the pictures from my head and *realize* them outside of me, between real pieces of furniture and real walls as bright and visible as those that flashed on the screens. But all in vain. I could no longer be blind to my double imposture: I was pretending to be an actor, pretending to be a hero.

Hardly did I begin to write than I laid down my pen to rejoice. The imposture was the same, but I have said that I regarded words as the

quintessence of things. Nothing disturbed me
more than to see my scrawls little by little change
their will-o'-the-wisp gleam for the dull consistency of matter: it was the realization of the imaginary. Caught in the trap of naming, a lion, a
captain of the Second Empire, or a Bedouin
would be brought into the dining room; they remained captive there forever, embodied in signs.
I thought I had anchored my dreams in the world
by the scratchings of a steel nib. I asked for and
was given a notebook and a bottle of purple ink.
I inscribed on the cover: "Novel Notebook." The
first story I completed was entitled *For a Butterfly*. A scientist, his daughter, and an athletic
young explorer sailed up the Amazon in search
of a precious butterfly. The argument, the characters, the particulars of the adventures, and
even the title were borrowed from a story in
pictures that had appeared in the preceding
quarter. This cold-blooded plagiarism freed me
from my remaining misgivings; everything was
necessarily true since I invented nothing. I did
not aspire to be published, but I had contrived to
be printed in advance, and I did not pen a line
that was not guaranteed by my model. Did I
take myself for an imitator? No, but for an orig-
inal author. I retouched, I livened things up. For
example, I was careful to change the names of
the characters. This slight tampering entitled me
to blend memory and imagination. New sen-

tences, already written, took shape in my head with the implacable sureness ascribed to inspiration. I transcribed them. They took on, beneath my eyes, the density of things. If, as is commonly believed, the inspired author is other than himself in the depths of his soul, I experienced inspiration between the ages of seven and eight.

I was never completely taken in by this "automatic writing." But I also enjoyed the game for its own sake. Being an only child, I could play it by myself. Now and then I would stop writing. I would pretend to hesitate, I would pucker my brow, assume a moonstruck expression, so as to feel I was a *writer*. I loved plagiarism, out of pretentiousness, be it added, and I deliberately carried it to an extreme, as will be seen presently.

Boussenard and Jules Verne did not miss an opportunity to be educational. At the most critical moments, they would break off the story to go into a description of a poisonous plant, of a native dwelling. As reader, I skipped these didactic passages; as author, I padded my novels with them. I meant to teach my contemporaries everything that I didn't know: the customs of the Fuegians, the flora of Africa, the climate of the desert. The collector of butterflies and his daughter, who had been separated by a stroke of fate and were then aboard the same ship without knowing it and victims of the same shipwreck, clung to the same life-buoy, raised their heads, and cried out: "Daisy!", "Papa!" Alas, a shark was on the prowl for fresh meat; it drew near; its belly shone in the waves. Would the unfortunate pair escape death? I went to get volume "Pr-Z" of the Big Larousse, carried it painfully to my desk, opened it to the right page, and, starting a new paragraph, copied out, word for word: "Sharks are common in the South Atlantic. These big sea-fish, which are very voracious, are sometimes forty feet long and weigh as much as eight tons . . ." I would take my time transcribing the article. I felt charmingly boring, as distinguished as Boussenard, and, not yet knowing how I was going to save my heroes, I would stew slowly in an exquisite trance.

This new activity was destined in every way to be an additional imitation. My mother was lavish with encouragement. She would bring visitors into the dining-room so that they could surprise the young creator at his school-desk. I pretended to be too absorbed to be aware of my admirers' presence. They would withdraw on tiptoe, whispering that I was too cute for words, that it was too-too charming. My uncle Emile gave me a little typewriter, which I didn't use. Mme. Picard bought me a globe so that I would make no mistakes in laying out my globetrotters' itinerary.

Anne Marie copied out my second novel, *The Banana-seller,* on glossy paper. It was shown about. "At least," she would say, "he behaves himself, he doesn't make any noise." Fortunately, the consecration was put off by my grandfather's displeasure.

Karl had never approved of what he called my "unwholesome reading-matter." When my mother informed him that I had begun to write, he was at first delighted, expecting, I suppose, an account of our family life with pungent observations and adorably naïve remarks. He took my notebook, leafed through it, scowled, and left the dining-room, furious at finding a repetition of the "nonsense" of my favorite gazettes. Eventually, he ignored my writings. My mother was mortified and tried several times to trick him into reading *The Banana-seller*. She would wait until he had put on his slippers and settled down in his armchair. While he rested silently, staring grimly ahead, with his hands in his lap, she would pick up my manuscript, leaf through it casually, and then, as if suddenly taken with it, would start laughing to herself. Finally, as if irresistibly carried away, she would hand it to my grandfather: "Do read it, Papa! It's *too* funny for words." But he would thrust the notebook aside, or, if he did glance at it, it was to point out, irritably, my spelling mistakes. In the course of time my

mother was intimidated. Not daring to congratulate me and afraid of hurting me, she stopped
reading my work so as not to have to talk to me
about it.

Ignored and barely tolerated, my literary activities became semi-clandestine. Nevertheless, I
continued them diligently, during recreation
periods, on Thursdays and Sundays, during
vacation, and, when I had the luck to be sick, in
bed. I remember happy convalescences and a
black, red-edged notebook which I would take up
and lay down like a tapestry. I "played movies"
less often; my novels took the place of everything. In short, I wrote for my own pleasure.

My plots grew complicated. I introduced the
most varied episodes, I indiscriminately poured
everything I read, good or bad, into these catch-
alls. The stories suffered as a result. Nevertheless, I gained thereby, for I had to join things up,
which meant inventing, and I consequently did
less plagiarizing. In addition, I split myself in
two. The year before, when I "played movies,"
I played my own role, I threw myself body and
soul into the imaginary, and I thought more than
once that I would be completely swallowed up in
it. As author, the hero was still myself; I projected my epic dreams upon him. All the same,

there were two of us: he did not have my name, and I referred to him only in the third person. Instead of endowing him with my gestures, I fashioned for him, by means of words, a body that I made an effort to see. This sudden "distancing" might have frightened me; it charmed me. I was delighted to be *him* without his quite being me. He was my doll, I could bend him to my whims, could pierce his side with a lance and then nurse and cure him the way my mother nursed and cured me. My favorite authors, who did have a certain sense of shame, stopped short of the sublime. Even in Zévaco, no valiant knight ever slew more than twenty knaves at a time. I wanted to change the adventure novel radically. I threw verisimilitude overboard. I multiplied enemies and dangers tenfold. In order to save his fiancée and future father-in-law, the young explorer in *For a Butterfly* fought the sharks for three days and three nights; in the end, the sea was red. The same character, wounded, escaped from a ranch that was besieged by Apaches, crossed the desert with his guts in his hands, and refused to let himself be sewn up before he spoke to the general. A little later, under the name of Goetz von Berlichingen, the same character routed an army. One against all: that was my rule. Let the source of this grim and grandiose reverie be sought in the bourgeois, puritan individualism of my environment.

As a hero, I fought against tyranny. As a demiurge, I became a tyrant myself. I experienced all the temptations of power. I was harmless, I became wicked. What prevented me from plucking Daisy's eyes out? Scared to death, I answered: nothing. And pluck them out I did, as I would have plucked off the wings of a fly. I wrote, with beating heart: "Daisy ran her hand over her eyes. She had become blind," and I sat there stunned, with my pen in the air. I had produced an event in the realm of the absolute that compromised me delightfully. I was not really sadistic: my perverse joy would immediately change into panic, I would annul all my decrees, I would cross them out over and over until they were indecipherable. The girl would regain her sight, or rather she had never lost it. But the memory of my caprices tormented me for a long time: I seriously worried myself.

The written word also worried me. At times, weary of mild massacres for children, I would let myself daydream; I would discover, in a state of anguish, ghastly possibilities, a monstrous universe that was only the underside of my omnipotence; I would say to myself: anything can happen! and that meant: I can imagine anything. Tremulously, always on the point of tearing up the page, I would relate supernatural atrocities. If my mother happened to read over my shoulder, she would utter a cry of glory and alarm: "What an imagination!" She would suck her lips, wanting to speak, and, finding nothing to say, would suddenly rush off. Her retreat heightened my anguish. But the imagination was not involved. I did not invent those horrors; I found them, like everything else, in my memory.

In that period, the western world was choking to death: that is what was called "the sweetness of living." For want of visible enemies, the bourgeoisie took pleasure in being scared of its own shadow. It exchanged its boredom for a directed anxiety. People spoke of spiritism, of ectoplasm. At 2 Rue le Goff, opposite our house, there were sessions of table turning. They took place on the fourth floor, "in the magician's apartment," as my grandmother put it. She would sometimes call us, and we would arrive in time to see pairs of hands on a pedestal table, but someone would come to the window and draw the curtains. Louise claimed that children of my age, accompanied by their mothers, visited the magician every day. "And," she said, "I see him. There's a laying on of hands." My grandfather would shake his head. Although he condemned those practices, he dared not make fun of them. My mother was afraid of them. My grandmother, for once, seemed more intrigued than sceptical. Finally they would all agree: "The main thing is not to get involved in it. It drives you crazy!" Fantastic stories were all the rage. High-minded newspapers dished out two or three a week to that dechristianized public which was nostalgic for the beauties of faith. The narrator would relate, in all objectivity, a disturbing fact. He would give positivism a chance. However strange the event might be, it had to entail a rational explanation. The author would seek this explanation, find it, and present it fairly. But at once he would cunningly make us realize how inadequate and slight it was. Nothing more: the account would end with a question. But that was enough; the Other World was there, all the more formidable in that it was not named.

When I opened *Le Matin,* I would be frozen with fear. One story in particular struck me. I still remember the title of it: "Wind in the Trees." One summer evening, a sick woman, alone on the first floor of a country house, is tossing about in bed. A chestnut tree pushes its branches into the room through the open window. On the ground floor, several persons are sitting and talking. They are watching darkness settle on the garden. Suddenly someone points to the chestnut tree: "Look at that! Can it be windy?" They are surprised. They go out on the porch. Not a breath of air. Yet the leaves are shaking. At that moment, a cry! The sick woman's husband rushes upstairs and finds his young wife sitting up in bed. She points to the tree and falls over dead. The tree is as quiet as ever. What did she see? A lunatic has escaped from the asylum. It must have been he, hidden in the tree, who showed his grinning face. It's he, it *must* be he, for the reason that no other explanation can be satisfactory. And yet . . . How is it that no one saw him go up or down? How is it that the dogs didn't bark? How could he have been arrested, six hours later, sixty miles from the estate? Questions without an answer. The writer starts a new paragraph and concludes casually: "According to the people of the village, it was Death that shook the branches of the chestnut tree." I threw the paper aside, stamped my foot, and cried aloud: "No! No!" My heart was bursting in my chest. One day, in a train going to Limoges, I thought I would faint as I turned the pages of the Hachette Almanac. I had come upon a drawing that was enough to make one's hair stand on end: a quay beneath the moon; a long gnarled claw came out of the water, took hold of a drunkard, and dragged him to the bottom. The picture illustrated a text that I read eagerly and that ended—or almost—with the following words: "Was it the hallucination of an alcoholic? Had Hell opened up?" I was afraid of the water, afraid of crabs and trees. Afraid of books in particular. I cursed the fiends who filled their stories with such atrocious figures. Yet I imitated them.

Of course, an occasion was necessary. For example, nightfall. The dining-room would be bathed in shadow. I would push my little desk against the window. The anguish would start creeping up again. The docility of my heroes, who were unfailingly sublime, unappreciated and rehabilitated, would reveal their unsubstantiality. Then *it* would come, a dizzying, invisible being that fascinated me. In order to be seen, it had to be described. I quickly finished off the adventure I was working on, took my characters to an entirely different part of the globe, generally subterranean or underseas, and hastily exposed them to new dangers: as improvised geologists or deep-sea divers, they would pick up the Being's trail, follow it, and suddenly encounter it. What flowed from my pen at that point—an octopus with eyes of flame, a twenty-ton crustacean, a giant spider that talked—was I myself, a child monster; it was my boredom with life, my fear of death, my dullness and my perversity. I did not recognize myself. No sooner was the foul creature born than it rose up against me, against my brave speleologists. I feared for their lives. My heart would race away; I would forget my hand; penning the words, I would think I was reading them. Very often things ended there: I wouldn't deliver the men up to the Beast, but I didn't get them out of trouble either. In short, it was enough that I had put them in contact. I would get up and go to the kitchen or the library. The next day, I would leave a page or two blank and launch my characters on a new venture. Strange "novels," always unfinished, always begun over or, if you like, continued under other titles, odds and ends of gloomy tales and cheery adventures, of fantastic events and encyclopedia articles. I have lost them and I sometimes think it's a pity. If it had occurred to me to lock them up, they would reveal to me my entire childhood.

I was beginning to find myself. I was almost nothing, at most an activity without content, but that was all that was needed. I was escaping from play-acting. I was not yet working, but I had already stopped playing. The liar was finding his truth in the elaboration of his lies. I was born of writing. Before that, there was only a play of mirrors. With my first novel I knew that a child had got into the hall of mirrors. By writing I was existing, I was escaping from the grown-ups, but I existed only in order to write, and if I said "I," that meant "I who write." In any case, I knew joy. The public child was making private appointments with himself.

It was too good to last. I would have remained sincere if I had stuck to my clandestine existence. But I was yanked away from it. I was reaching the age when bourgeois children were supposed

to show the first signs of their vocation. We had
been informed long before that my Schweitzer
cousins, in Guérigny, would be engineers, like
their father. There was not another minute to
lose. Mme. Picard wanted to be the first to discover the sign I bore on my brow. "The child will
be a writer," she said with conviction. Louise,
much annoyed, responded with her curt little
smile. Blanche Picard turned to her and repeated
sternly: "He'll be a writer! He's meant to be a
writer." My mother knew that Charles was not
very encouraging. She was afraid of complications and looked at me closely. "You think so,
Blanche? You think so?" But in the evening, as
I jumped up and down on my bed, in my nightshirt, she hugged my shoulders hard and said with
a smile: "My little man will be a writer!" My
grandfather was informed very cautiously. An
outburst was feared. He merely nodded, and the
following Thursday I heard him say confi-
dentially to M. Simonnot that in the evening of
life no one could witness the budding of a talent
without being thrilled. He continued to pay no
attention to my scribbling, but when his German
pupils came to dine at the house, he would place
his hand on my skull and repeat, separating the
syllables so as not to miss an opportunity to teach
them French locutions by the direct method: "He
has the bump of literature."

He didn't believe a word of what he said, but what of it? The harm was done. Had he been dead set against me, he might only have made matters worse. I might have stuck to my guns obstinately. Karl proclaimed my vocation in order to be able to divert me from it. He was the opposite of a cynic, but he was growing old; his enthusiasms tired him. I am sure that deep down, in a cold desert zone which he seldom visited, *he* knew what to think about me, the family, and himself. One day, as I lay reading between his feet, during one of the endless silences he imposed on us, he was suddenly struck by an idea that made him forget my presence. He looked at my mother reproachfully: "And what if he got it into his head to live by his pen?" My grandfather appreciated Verlaine, of whom he had a volume of selected poems. But he thought he had seen him enter a bar in 1894 "as drunk as a pig." That encounter had thoroughly confirmed his contempt for professional writers; they were mere miracle-mongers who asked for a gold-piece to show you the moon and ended by showing you their behind for five francs. My mother looked frightened but didn't answer. She knew that Charles had other plans for me. In most of the lycées, the teachers of German were Alsatians who had chosen France and who had been given their posts in reward for their patriotism. Caught between two nations, between two languages, their studies had been somewhat irregular, and there were gaps in their culture. That made them suffer. They also complained that they were left out of things in the academic community because of their colleagues' hostility. I would be their avenger; I would avenge my grandfather. Grandson of an Alsatian, I was at the same time a Frenchman of France. Karl would help me acquire universal knowledge. I would take the royal road: in my person, martyred Alsace would enter the Ecole Normale Supérieure, would pass the teaching examination with flying colors, and would become that prince, a teacher of letters. One evening he announced that he wanted to talk to me man to man. The women withdrew. He sat me down on his lap and spoke to me very seriously. I would be a writer, that was understood, I knew him well enough not to fear that he would oppose my wishes. But I had to know exactly what I was in for: literature did not fill a man's belly. Did I know that famous writers had died of hunger? That others had sold themselves in order to eat? If I wanted to remain independent, I would do well to choose a second profession. Teaching gave a man leisure. Scholarly interests went hand in hand with those of men of letters. I would move back and forth from one priestly function to the other. I would live in close contact with the great writers. At one and the same time,

I would reveal their works to my pupils and draw upon them for inspiration. I would beguile my provincial solitude by composing poems, by translating Horace into blank verse. I would write short literary articles for the local papers, a brilliant essay on the teaching of Greek for the *Pedagogic Review,* another on the psychology of adolescents. Upon my death, unpublished works would be found among my papers, a meditation on the sea, a one-act comedy, a few sensitive and scholarly pages on the monuments of Aurillac, enough to fill a thin volume that would be edited by former pupils.

For some time now, my grandfather's raptures over my virtues left me cold. I still pretended to listen to the voice that trembled with love when it called me a "gift from heaven," but I stopped hearing it. Why did I listen to it that day, when it lied to me most deliberately? As a result of what misunderstanding did I make it say the opposite of what it claimed to be teaching me? The fact is that it had changed: it had dried and hardened, and I took it for that of the absent father who had begotten me. Charles had two faces: when he played grandfather, I regarded him as a buffoon of my own kind and did not respect him. But when he spoke to M. Simonnot or to his sons, when he made the women wait on him at table, by pointing, without a word, at the oil and vinegar cruets or the bread-basket, I admired his authority. I was particularly impressed by the play of his forefinger: he would be careful not to point, but would move it vaguely in the air, half bent, so that the designation remained imprecise and the two servants had to guess at his orders. At times, in exasperation, my grandmother would make a mistake and hand him the fruit-bowl when he asked for wine. I would lay the blame on my grandmother. I deferred to these royal desires that wished to be anticipated more than to be satisfied. If Charles had flung his arms wide open and cried out from afar: "Here comes the new Hugo, here's a budding Shakespeare!", I would now be an industrial draughtsman or a teacher of literature. He was careful not to. For the first time, I was dealing with the patriarch. He seemed forbidding and all the more venerable in that he had forgotten to adore me. He was Moses dictating the new law. My law. He had mentioned my vocation only in order to point out its disadvantages. I concluded that he took it for granted. Had he predicted that my pages would be drenched with tears or that I would roll on the rug, my bourgeois restraint would have been shocked. He convinced me of my vocation by giving me to understand that such showy disorders were not in store for me: in order to discuss Aurillac or pedagogy, there was no need, alas, of fever or tumult. Others would heave

the immortal sobs of the twentieth century. I
resigned myself to never being thunder or lightning; I would shine in literature by virtue of my
domestic qualities, my amiability, my steadiness.
The craft of writing appeared to me as an adult
activity, so ponderously serious, so trifling, and,
at bottom, so lacking in interest that I didn't
doubt for a moment that it was in store for me. I
said to myself both "that's all it is" and "I'm
gifted." Like all dreamers, I confused disenchant-
ment with truth.

Karl had turned me inside out like a rabbit
skin. I had thought I was going to write only in
order to set down my dreams, whereas, if I were
to believe him, I dreamed only in order to exercise my pen. My anguish and imaginary passions
were only the ruses of my talent; their sole function was to send me back to my desk every day
and provide me with narrative themes suitable to
my age while I awaited the great dictations of
experience and maturity. I lost my fabulous illusions. "Ah!" my grandfather would say, "it's
not enough to have eyes. You must learn to use
them. Do you know what Flaubert did when de
Maupassant was a little boy? He sat him down in
front of a tree and gave him two hours to describe it." I therefore learned to see. As a predestined singer of the glories of Aurillac, I would
gaze with melancholy at those other monuments:

the blotter, the piano, the clock which would also be immortalized—why not—by my future lucubrations. I observed. It was a dismal and disappointing game: I had to stand in front of the stamped velvet armchair and inspect it. What was there to say about it? Well, that it was covered with fuzzy green material, that it had two arms, four legs, a back surmounted by two little wooden pine-cones. That was all for the moment, but I would come back to it, I would do better next time, I would end by knowing it inside out. Later, I would describe it; my readers would say: "How well observed it is, how accurately! It's exactly right! That's the kind of thing one doesn't invent!" Depicting real objects with real words that were penned with a real pen, I'd be hanged if I didn't become real myself! In short, I knew once and for all what to answer the ticket-collectors who asked me for my ticket.

One can well imagine that I appreciated my good fortune! The trouble was that I didn't enjoy it. My appointment had been confirmed, I had very kindly been given a future, and I openly declared it was delightful, but I secretly loathed it. Had I asked for that clerk's job? Associating with great men had convinced me that one could not be a writer without becoming illustrious. But when I compared the glory that had befallen me with the few scanty booklets I would leave behind, I felt I had been fooled. Could I really believe that my grand-nephews would re-read me and be enthusiastic about so slight an output, about subjects that bored me in advance? I sometimes told myself that I would be saved from oblivion by my "style," that enigmatic virtue which my grandfather denied Stendhal and recognized in Renan. But those meaningless words did not succeed in reassuring me.

Above all, I had to renounce my own self. Two months earlier I had been a swashbuckler, an athlete. That was over! I was being called upon to choose between Corneille and Pardaillan. I dismissed Pardaillan, whom I really and truly loved; out of humility, I decided in favor of Corneille. I had seen heroes running and fighting in the Luxembourg. Staggered by their beauty, I had realized that I belonged to the lesser breed. I had to proclaim the fact, to sheathe my sword, to go back to the common herd, to resume relations with the great writers, those little squirts who didn't intimidate me. They had been rickety children; at least I resembled them in that. They had become sickly adults, rheumy old men; I would resemble them in that. A nobleman had had Voltaire beaten, and I perhaps would be horsewhipped by a captain, a former park bully.

I felt gifted out of resignation. In Charles Schweitzer's study, amidst worn, torn, battered books, talent was what was valued least of all. Similarly, under the Old Regime, many a younger son who was doomed by birth to the priesthood would have sold his soul to command a battalion. The dismal pomp of fame was long epitomized for me by the following scene: on a long table covered with a white cloth were pitchers of orangeade and bottles of sparkling wine; I took a glass; men in evening clothes who surrounded me—there were a good fifteen of them—drank a toast to my health; I could sense behind us the bare, dusty vastness of a hired hall. It's obvious that I expected nothing more from life than that it revive for me, late in life, the annual party of the Modern Language Institute.

Thus, in the course of discussions that were repeated over and over, my destiny was being shaped at number one Rue le Goff, in a fifth-floor apartment, below Goethe and Schiller, above Molière, Racine, and La Fontaine, on a par with Heinrich Heine and Victor Hugo. Karl and I would send the women away; we would hug each other tightly; we would continue at close range that deaf men's dialogue, each word of which left its mark on me. By deft little strokes Charles convinced me that I wasn't a genius. Indeed I wasn't, I knew it, I didn't give a damn. Heroism, absent and impossible, was the sole object of my passion, heroism, the blazing flame of the poor in spirit. My inner poverty and the feeling of being gratuitous did not allow me to renounce it entirely. I no longer dared be enraptured by my future gesture, but at bottom I was terrorized. Someone must have been mistaken about the child or the vocation. Since I was lost, I accepted, in obedience to Karl, the studious career of a writer. In short, he drove me into literature by the care he took to divert me from it, to such an extent that even now I sometimes wonder, when I am in a bad mood, whether I have not consumed so many days and nights, covered so many pages with ink, thrown on the market so many books that nobody wanted, solely in the mad hope of pleasing my grandfather. That would be a farce. At the age of more than fifty, I would find myself engaged, in order to carry out the will of a man long dead, in an undertaking which he would not have failed to repudiate.

The fact is that I resemble Swann when he has gotten over his love: "To think," he sighs, "that I messed up my life for a woman who wasn't my type!" At times, I'm secretly a skunk; it's a matter of elementary hygiene. Now, the skunk is always right, but up to a certain point. It's true that I'm not a gifted writer. I've been told so, I've been called labored. So I am; my books reek of sweat and effort; I grant that they stink in the nostrils of our aristocrats. I've often written them against myself, which means against everybody,* with an intentness of mind that has ended by becoming high blood pressure. My commandments were sewn into my skin; if I go a day without writing, the scar burns me; if I write too easily, it also burns me. This simple-minded exigency still acts upon me by its rigidity, its clumsiness. It resembles the solemn, prehistoric crabs that the ocean throws up on the beaches of Long Island. Like them, it is a survival of a bygone era. For a long time, I envied the concierges of the Rue Lacépède sitting astride their chairs when summer evenings brought them out on the sidewalk. Their innocent eyes saw without being commissioned to look.

But the fact is this: apart from a few old men who dip their pens in eau de Cologne and little dandies who write like butchers, all writers have to sweat. That's due to the nature of the Word: one speaks in one's own language, one writes in a foreign language. I conclude from this that we're all alike in our profession: we're all galley-slaves, we're all tattooed. Besides, the reader has realized that I loathe my childhood and whatever has survived of it. I wouldn't listen to my grand-

---

* Be self-indulgent, and those who are also self-indulgent will like you. Tear your neighbor to pieces, and the other neighbors will laugh. But if you beat your soul, all souls will cry out.

father's voice, that recorded voice which wakes me with a start and drives me to my table, if it were not my own, if, between the ages of eight and ten, I had not arrogantly assumed responsibility for the supposedly imperative mandate that I had received in all humility.

> *"I quite realize that I am only a machine*
> *which makes books."*   (Chateaubriand)

I almost gave up. In the last analysis, all that I saw in the gift to which Karl paid lip-service, deeming it unwise to deny it entirely, was a matter of chance that was unable to legitimize that other matter of chance, myself. My mother had a beautiful voice; *therefore* she sang. She nevertheless didn't travel without a ticket. I had the bump of literature; therefore I would write, I would work that vein all my life. Well and good. But Art lost—at least for me—its sacred powers. I would remain a vagabond—with a little more security, that was all. In order for me to feel necessary, someone would have had to express a need for me. My family had been feeding me that illusion for some time; they had told me again and again that I was a gift of heaven, that I had been eagerly awaited, that I was indispensable to my grandfather, to my mother. I no longer believed it, but I did continue to feel that one is born superfluous unless one is brought into the world with the special purpose of fulfilling an expectation. My pride and forlornness were such at the time that I wished I were dead or that I were needed by the whole world.

I had stopped writing. Mme. Picard's declarations had given such importance to the soliloquies of my pen that I no longer dared to continue them. When I wanted to go back to my novel, to save at least the young couple that I had left in the middle of the Sahara Desert with neither provisions nor helmets, I suffered the horrors of impotence. No sooner was I seated than my head filled with fog. I chewed at my nails and frowned: I had lost my innocence. I got up and prowled about the apartment with the soul of an incendiary. Unfortunately, I never set fire to it. Docile by virtue of circumstances, by taste, by custom, I came to rebellion later only because I had carried submission to an extreme. I was given a "homework notebook" with a cloth cover and red edges. No external sign distinguished it from my "novel notebook." As soon as I looked at it, my school work and my personal obligations merged; I identified the author with the pupil, the pupil with the future teacher. The act of writing and the teaching of grammar came to one and the same thing. My pen, which had been socialized, dropped from my hand, and several months went by without my picking it up. My grandfather smiled in his beard whenever I dragged my sullenness into his study. He no doubt thought to himself that his policy was bearing its first fruits.

It failed because I had an epic mind. Thrown back among the commoners, with my sword broken, I often had the following anxiety dream: I was in the Luxembourg, near the pond, facing the Senate Building. I had to protect a blond little girl from an unknown danger; she resembled Vévé, who had died a year earlier. The girl looked up at me calmly and confidently with her serious eyes. Often she was holding a hoop. It was I who was frightened: I was afraid of abandoning her to invisible forces. But how I loved her, with how mournful a love! I still love her. I have looked for her, lost her, found her again, held her in my arms, lost her again: she is the Epic. At the age of eight, just as I was about to resign myself, I pulled myself together; in order to save that dead little girl, I launched out upon a simple and mad operation that shifted the course of my life: I palmed off on the writer the sacred powers of the hero.

At the source of this was a discovery, or rather a reminiscence, for I had had a foreboding of it two years earlier: great writers are akin to knights-errant in that both elicit passionate signs of gratitude. In the case of Pardaillan, no further proof was needed: the back of his hand was furrowed with the tears of fair orphans. But if I was to believe the encyclopedia and the obituaries that I read in the newspapers, the writer was not less favored: if only he lived long enough, he invariably ended by receiving a letter from an unknown person who *thanked him.* From then on, thanks kept pouring in; they piled up on his desk, cluttered his home; foreigners crossed the seas to pay tribute to him; his fellow-countrymen took up a collection after his death to erect a monument to him; in his native town and sometimes in the capital of his country, streets were named after him. In themselves, these gratifications did not interest me; they reminded me too much of the family playacting. There was, however, a certain drawing that staggered me: the famous novelist Dickens is going to land in New York in a few hours; the ship on which he is sailing can be seen in the distance; the crowd is gathered on the pier to welcome him; it opens all its mouths and waves a thousand caps; it is so dense that children are suffocating; yet it is lonely, an orphan and a widow, depopulated by the mere absence of the man for whom it is waiting. I murmured: "There's someone missing here. It's Dickens!", and my eyes filled with tears. However, I brushed aside the effects and went straight to their cause:

in order to be so wildly acclaimed, I thought to myself, men of letters must face the greatest dangers and render the most distinguished service to mankind. Once in my life I had witnessed a similar burst of enthusiasm: hats went flying, men and women cried "bravo," "hurray;" it was a July 14th; the Algerian riflemen were parading by. This memory finally convinced me: despite their physical defects, their primness, their seeming femininity, writers risked their lives as free lances in mysterious combats; their military courage was applauded even more than their talent. "So it's true," I said to myself, "they're *needed*!" In Paris, in New York, in Moscow, they are awaited, with anguish or ecstasy, before they have published their first book, before they have begun to write, even before they are born.

But then . . . what about me? Me, whose mission it was to write? Well, they were waiting for me. I transformed Corneille into Pardaillan: he retained his bandy legs, narrow chest, and dismal face, but I took away his avarice and love of lucre; I deliberately blended the art of writing and generosity. After that, it was the easiest thing in the world to change myself into Corneille and to confer upon myself the mandate of protecting the race. My new imposture was preparing me for an odd future. For the moment, I had everything to gain by it. I had been born with disadvantages, and have spoken of my efforts to be born over: entreaties of innocence in jeopardy had called me forth a thousand times. But it was all in fun: fake knight that I was, I performed fake exploits, the hollowness of which finally disgusted me. But my dreams were now being given back to me and were becoming real. For my vocation *was* real; I could have no doubt about it, since the high priest vouched for it. I, the imaginary child, was becoming a true paladin whose exploits would be real books. I was being summoned! People were awaiting my work, the first volume of which, despite my zeal, would not come out before 1935. Around 1930, people would start losing patience: "He's certainly taking his time! He's been living off the fat of the land for twenty-five years! Are we going to die without reading him?" I would answer with my 1913 voice: "Say! Let me have time to work!" But nicely. I could see that they needed my help —only God knew why—and that this need had begotten me, me, the only means of satisfying it. I strove to catch a glimpse, deep inside me, of that universal expectation, my gushing spring and my reason for living. I would sometimes feel I was about to succeed, and then, after a moment, I would drop the whole business. In any case, those false illuminations were enough for me. I looked out, reassured: perhaps I was already being missed in certain places. But no, it was too soon. I was the bright object of a desire that was still unborn, and I gladly consented to remain incognito for a while. At times, my grandmother would take me with her to her circulating library, and it would amuse me to see tall, pensive, unsatisfied ladies gliding from wall to wall in search of the author who would satisfy them: he was not to be found, since he was I, that youngster who was standing under their very noses and whom they didn't even look at.

I would laugh slyly, I would weep tenderly. I had spent my short life inventing tastes and purposes for myself, but they were immediately watered down. But now my depths had been sounded and the plummet had touched rock-bottom; I was a writer as Charles Schweitzer was a grandfather, by birth and forever. Yet at times, beneath the enthusiasm, was a lurking anxiety: I refused to regard my talent, which I thought was guaranteed by Karl, as an accident, and I contrived to make a mandate of it, but for want of encouragement and a true demand for it, I was unable to forget that it was I who had conferred it upon myself. Looming up out of an antediluvian world just when I was escaping from Nature and at last becoming myself, that Other whom I was aspiring to be in the eyes of others, I faced my Destiny and recognized it: it was only my freedom; it had been set up be-

fore me by my own efforts as if it were a foreign
power. In short, I did not quite manage to
pigeon-hole myself. Nor to undeceive myself. I
wavered. My hesitation revived an old problem:
how to combine the certainties of Michael Strogoff and the generosity of Pardaillan. As a
knight, I had never taken orders from the king.
Was I to consent to being an author by command? The anxiety never lasted very long; I
was torn between two conflicting mystiques, but
I easily came to terms with their contradictions.
It even served my purposes to be both a gift of
heaven and a self-made man. When I was in a
good mood, everything derived from myself. I
had pulled myself up out of nothingness by my
own bootstraps in order to provide men with
the writings they wanted. In hours of gloom,
when I felt the sickening dullness of my good-
will, the only way of pulling myself together
was to lay stress on predestination: I would
summon the human race and foist on it the responsibility for my life; I was only the product
of a collective demand. Most of the time, I
managed to maintain my peace of mind by being
careful never to exclude entirely either the freedom that exalts or the necessity that justifies.

Pardaillan and Strogoff were able to get on
with each other: the danger lay elsewhere, and
I was made to witness an unpleasant encounter

that later obliged me to be wary. The one who was mainly responsible was Zévaco, whom I did not distrust. Was he trying to cramp my style or warn me? The fact is that one day, at a *posada* in Madrid, when I had eyes only for Pardaillan, who, poor chap, was resting and drinking a well-earned glass of wine, the author drew my attention to a customer who was none other than Cervantes. The two men get into a conversation, express their mutual esteem, and decide to carry out a virtuous attack together. Worse still, Cervantes, who is thoroughly delighted, confides to his new friend that he wants to write a book: until then, the main character was still nebulous, but, thank God, Pardaillan has appeared and would serve as a model. I was filled with indignation, I almost flung the book away: what a lack of tact! I was a writer-knight, I was being split in two, each half became a whole man, encountered the other, and challenged his existence. Pardaillan was not a fool but would not have written *Don Quixote*; Cervantes was a good fighter but couldn't be expected to rout twenty henchmen all by himself. Their friendship itself attested to their limits. The former thought: "He's somewhat puny, the bookworm, but he doesn't lack courage." And the latter: "By thunder! The trooper has a head on his shoulders." And besides, I didn't at all like the fact that my hero was being used as a model for the Knight of the Woeful Countenance. At the time when I "played movies," I had been given an expurgated *Don Quixote*; I had not read more than fifty pages of it: it publicly ridiculed my doughty deeds! And here was Zévaco himself . . . Whom could I trust? The truth is that I was a loose wench, a girl for soldiers: my heart, my cowardly heart, preferred the adventurer to the intellectual; I was ashamed to be only Cervantes. To prevent myself from betraying, I launched a reign of terror in my head and in my vocabulary; I persecuted the word heroism and its substitutes, I drove back the knights-errant, I talked to myself constantly about men of letters, about the risks they ran, about their sharp pens that ran the wicked through and through. I continued reading *Pardaillan and Fausta, Les Misérables, The Legend of the Centuries,* I wept over Jean Valjean, over Eviradnus, but once the book was shut I blotted their names from my memory and called upon my true regiment: Sylvio Pellico, imprisoned for life; André Chénier, guillotined; Etienne Dolet, burned at the stake; Byron, died for Greece. I strove with cold passion to transfigure my vocation by pouring into it my former dreams. Nothing daunted me. I twisted ideas, I falsified the meanings of words, I cut myself off from the world for fear of comparisons and of meeting the wrong people. The vacancy in my soul was followed by a total and permanent mobilization: I became a military dictator.

The anxiety persisted in another form. I sharpened my talent, well and good. But what purpose would it serve? Human beings needed me: *to do what?* I had the misfortune to question myself about my role and destination. I asked: "Well, what's it all about?", and I thought then and there that all was lost. It was about *nothing*. Wanting to be a hero is not enough. Neither courage nor the gift suffices; there must be hydras and dragons. There were none in sight. Voltaire and Rousseau had slashed about them in their day: the reason was that there still were tyrants. From his exile in Guernsey, Hugo had thundered against Badinguet, whom my grandfather had taught me to hate. But I found no merit in proclaiming my hatred, since that emperor had been dead for forty years. About contemporary history Charles said nothing. Though he was pro-Dreyfus, he never spoke to me about the affair. What a pity! The gusto with which I would have played the role of Zola: jostled and insulted as I leave the courtroom, I turn around on the running board of my carriage, I thrash the most aggressive—no, no: I find a terrible phrase that makes them draw back. And, of course, *I* refuse to flee to England; unappreciated, forsaken, what a thrill to be Griselda again, to tramp the streets of Paris without suspecting for a minute that the Pantheon awaits me.

My grandmother received *Le Matin* every day and, if I am not mistaken, *L'Excelsior*. I learned of the existence of the underworld, which I loathed, like all right-thinking people. But those tigers with human faces did not suit my purpose: the dauntless M. Lépine was able to handle them by himself. At times, workers got angry, capital immediately went down the drain, but I knew nothing about the matter, and I still don't know what my grandfather thought of it. He would cast his vote faithfully and emerge from the booth rejuvenated and a little smug, and when our women teased him: "Come on, tell us whom you voted for!", he would answer curtly: "That's a man's business!" Yet, when a new President of the Republic was elected, he gave us to understand, in a moment of abandon, that he deplored the candidacy of Pams: "He's a cigarette salesman!" he exclaimed angrily. That petty bourgeois intellectual wanted the chief civil-servant of France to be one of his peers, an intellectual petty bourgeois, Poincaré. My mother vouches for the fact that he voted Radical Socialist and that she knew it very well. It doesn't surprise me: he had chosen the civil-servants' party. And besides, the Radical Socialists had already outlived their usefulness: Charles had the satisfaction of voting for a party that stood for order by giving his vote to the party that supposedly was progressive. In short, French politics, as he saw it, was not at all in a bad way.

That cut me to the heart. I had armed myself to defend mankind against terrible dangers, and everyone assured me that it was quietly on its way to perfection. Grandfather had brought me up to respect bourgeois democracy; I would have gladly unsheathed my pen for it. But with de Fallières as President, the peasant voted: what more could I ask? And what does a republican do if he has the luck to live in a republic? He twiddles his thumbs, or else he teaches Greek and describes the monuments of Aurillac in his spare time. I was back where I had started from, and I thought I would stifle in that world without conflicts which left the writer unemployed.

Once again it was Charles who came to the rescue. Unwittingly, of course. Two years before, in an effort to awaken me to the spirit of humanism, he had set forth certain ideas about which he no longer said a word for fear of encouraging my folly but which had remained graven in my mind. They quietly regained their virulence and, in order to save what was essential, little by little transformed the writer-knight into a writer-martyr. I have spoken of how that minister manqué, faithful to his father's will, had retained the Divine and invested it in Culture. The product of that amalgam was the Holy Ghost, patron of arts and letters, of dead and modern languages, and of the Direct Method, a white dove that gratified the Schweitzer family with its apparitions, that fluttered, on Sundays, over organs and orchestras and perched, on working days, on my grandfather's head. Karl's earlier remarks assembled in my head and composed a discourse: the world was a prey to Evil; there was only one way of salvation: to die to one's self and to the World, to contemplate the impossible Ideas from the vantage point of a wreckage. As that could not be done without difficult and dangerous training, the job had been assigned to a body of specialists. The priesthood took mankind in hand and saved it by the reversibility of merits: the wild beasts of the temporal, large and small, had full leisure to kill each other or to live a dazed and truthless existence, since writers and artists meditated for them on Goodness and Beauty. In order to rescue the entire species from animality, only two conditions were required: that the relics of dead clerks—paintings, books, statues—be preserved in guarded places; that there remain at least one living clerk to carry on with the job and manufacture future relics.

Filthy twaddle: I gulped it down without quite understanding it; I still believed in it at the age of twenty. Because of it I regarded works of art for a long time as metaphysical events, the birth of which affected the universe. I dug up that fierce religion and made it mine in order to gild my dull vocation. I absorbed grudges and rancors that belonged neither to me nor my grandfather. The old bile of Flaubert, of the Goncourts, of Gautier poisoned me. Their abstract hatred of human beings, which entered me disguised as love, infected me with new pretensions. I became a Catharian, I confused literature with prayer, I made a human sacrifice of it. My brothers, I decided, were quite simply asking me to devote my pen to their redemption. They suffered from an insufficiency of being which, were it not for the intercession of the Saints, would have doomed them permanently to destruction. If I opened my eyes every morning, if, when I ran to the window, I saw still living Ladies and Gentlemen passing in the street, it was because a man working in a room had struggled from twilight to dawn to write an immortal page that earned us that one-day reprieve. He would start again at nightfall, this evening, tomorrow, until he died of exhaustion. I would carry on for him: I too would keep the race alive, at the edge of the abyss, by my mystic offering, by my work. The soldier quietly gave way to the priest: I, a tragic Parsifal, was offering myself up as an expiatory victim. The day I discovered Chanticleer, a knot was formed in my heart, a tangle of snakes that it took me thirty years to disentangle: thrashed, lacerated, and bleeding, that rooster finds a way of protecting a whole barnyard; his song is enough to put the hawk to flight, and the base throng showers praise on him after having jeered at him. With the hawk gone, the poet returns to the fray; Beauty inspires him, multiplies his strength tenfold; he pounces upon his adversary and downs him. I wept; Griselda, Corneille, and Pardaillan blended into one: Chanticleer would be *me*. It all looked simple: to write is to add a pearl to the Muses' necklace, to leave to posterity the memory of a model life, to defend the people against itself and its enemies, to bring down upon men, by means of a solemn Mass, the blessing of heaven. It did not occur to me that one could write in order to be read.

One writes for one's neighbors or for God. I decided to write for God with the purpose of saving my neighbors. I wanted gratitude and not readers. Scorn corrupted my generosity. During the period in which I was protecting female orphans, I had already begun to get rid of them by sending them into hiding. As a writer, my manner did not change: before saving mankind, I would start by blindfolding it; only then would

I turn against the black, swift little henchmen, against words; when my new orphan dared untie the blindfold, I would be far away. Saved by a lone deed, at first she would not notice, shining on a shelf in the National Library, the brand new little volume that bore my name.

I plead extenuating circumstances. There were three of them. Firstly, by means of this transparent fantasy I was questioning my right to live. In the mankind without a visa which awaits the Artist's good pleasure, one can easily recognize the coddled child who is bored on his perch; I accepted the loathsome myth of the Saint who saves the populace because, in the last analysis, the populace was myself: I declared myself a licensed redeemer of crowds so as to win my own salvation on the sly and, as the Jesuits say, into the bargain.

Secondly, I was nine years old. As an only child and without a friend, I did not imagine that my isolation could end. I must admit that I was a very unknown author. I had started writing again. My new novels, for want of anything better, resembled the old in every single way, but no one noticed it. Not even I, who hated to re-read myself. My pen raced away so fast that often my wrist ached. I would throw the filled notebooks on the floor, I would eventually forget about them, they would disappear. For that reason, I never finished anything: what was the good of relating the end of a story when the beginning was lost? Besides, if Karl had deigned to glance at those pages, I would not have regarded him as a *reader* but as a supreme judge, and I would have feared that he might condemn me. Writing, my grim labor, had no reference to anything and was thus an end in itself: I wrote in order to write. I don't regret it: had I been read, I would have tried to please, I would have become a wonder again. Being clandestine, I was true.

In any case, the idealism of the clerk was based on the realism of the child. I said earlier that as a result of discovering the world through language, for a long time I took language for the world. To exist was to have an official title somewhere on the infinite Tables of the Word; to write was to engrave new beings upon them or—and this was my most persistent illusion—to catch living things in the trap of phrases: if I combined words ingeniously, the object would get tangled up in the signs, I would have a hold on it. I began, in the Luxembourg, by focusing my attention on a bright simulacrum of a plane-tree. I did not observe it. Quite the contrary: I trusted to the void, I waited. A moment later, its true foliage would suddenly appear in the form of a simple adjective or, at times, of a whole proposition: I had enriched the universe with quivering greenery. Never did I set my finds down on paper: they were being stored away, so I thought, in my memory. Actually, I would forget them. But they gave me an inkling of my future role: I would impose names. For centuries, in Aurillac, idle heaps of whiteness had been begging for definite contours, for a meaning; I would make real monuments of them. As a terrorist, I was concerned only with their being: I would establish it by means of language. As a rhetorician, I cared only for words: I would set up cathedrals of words beneath the blue eyes of the word sky. I would build for the ages. When I took up a book, I could see that though I opened it and shut it twenty times, it did not deteriorate. Gliding over that incorruptible substance, the *text,* my gaze was merely a tiny, surface accident; it did not disturb anything, did not wear anything away. I, on the other hand, passive and ephemeral, was a dazzled mosquito, pierced by the rays of a beacon. I would put out the light and leave the study: invisible in the darkness, the book kept sparkling, for itself alone. I would give my works the violence of those corrosive flashes, and later, in ruined libraries, they would outlive man.

I enjoyed my obscurity, I wanted to prolong it, to make a merit of it. I envied the famous prisoners who wrote in dungeon cells on candle paper. They had respected their obligation to redeem their contemporaries and had lost that of associating with them. Of course, moral progress had reduced my chance of drawing on confinement for my talent, but I didn't lose all hope: impressed by the modesty of my ambitions, Providence would set its heart on fulfilling them. While waiting, I locked myself up in advance.

Thwarted by my grandfather, my mother took every opportunity to depict my future joys. In her effort to give me pleasure, she put into my life everything that was lacking in her own: tranquillity, leisure, harmony. I was a young teacher, still unmarried; a charming old lady would rent me a comfortable room that smelled of lavender and fresh linen; I would pop over to the lycée, I would pop back; in the evening, I would linger at the threshold of my door to chat with my landlady, who doted upon me; besides, everybody loved me, because I was courteous and well bred. I would hear only one word: your room. I would forget about the lycée, the officer's widow, the provincial smell; all I saw was a ring of light on my table: in the middle of a room that was drowned in shadow, I would be bending over a cloth notebook. My mother would go on with her story, would skip ten years: a superintendent of schools protected me, the good society of Aurillac was glad to receive me, my young wife loved me tenderly, we would have beautiful, healthy children, two boys and a girl, she would inherit money, I would buy a piece of land on the outskirts of town, we would build a house, and every Sunday the whole family would go to see how it was coming along. I listened to none of this: during those ten years, I had not left my table. Short, with a moustache, like my father, I sat perched on a pile of dictionaries; my moustache was turning white, my wrist raced away, the note-books dropped to the floor, one after the other. Mankind was sleeping, it was night-time; my wife and children were sleeping, unless they were dead; my landlady was sleeping. Sleep had blotted me from all memories. What solitude! Two billion men horizontal, and I, above them, alone on the watch-tower.

The Holy Ghost was observing me. It so hap-pened that he had just reached a decision to return to Heaven and abandon human beings; I had just about time enough to offer myself; I showed him the wounds of my soul, the tears that drenched my paper; he looked over my shoulder and read, and his anger subsided. Was he ap-peased by the depth of my suffering or by the magnificence of the work? I said to myself: by the work, but secretly thought: by the suffering. Of course, the Holy Ghost appreciated only what was really artistic, but I had read de Musset, I knew that "the most despairing songs are the loveliest," and I had decided to capture Beauty by a decoy-despair. The word genius had always seemed suspect to me: I went so far as to conceive a loathing for it. Where would the anguish be, where the ordeal, where the foiled temptation, where, in short, the merit, if I possessed the gift? It was bad enough that I had a body and that I had the same face every day; I wasn't going to let myself be confined in a given framework. I accepted my appointment on condition that it be based on nothing, that it shine gratuitously in the absolute void. The Holy Ghost and I held secret meetings: "You'll write," he said to me. I wrung my hands: "What is there about me, Lord, that has made you choose me?"—"Nothing in particular."—"Then, why me?"—"For no reason."—"Do I at least have an aptitude for writing?"—"Not at all. Do you think that the great works are born of flowing pens?"— "Lord, since I'm such a non-entity, how could I write a book?"—"By buckling down to it."—"Does that mean anyone can write?"—"Anyone. But you're the one I've chosen." This faking was very convenient: it enabled me to proclaim my insignificance and at the same time to venerate in me the author of future masterpieces. I was elected, branded, but without talent: everything would come from my sorrows and long patience. I refused myself any singularity: traits of character make one stiff

and awkward. I was faithful to nothing but the
royal commitment that was leading me to glory
by way of torment. The torments remained to be
found. That was the one and only problem, but
it seemed insoluble since I had been deprived of
the hope of living in poverty: whether I was
obscure or famous, I drew a salary on the Education Budget; I would never go hungry. I promised myself pangs of love and heartaches, but
without enthusiasm: I loathed anguished lovers.
I was shocked by Cyrano, that fake Pardaillan
who talked silly nonsense to women: the real one
dragged all hearts in his wake without even
noticing it, though it's only fair to say that the
death of Violetta, his sweetheart, had broken
his heart forever. I could, of course, be a widower,
with an incurable ache: because of a woman but
through no fault of hers. That would allow me
to reject the advances of all the others. The idea
was worth considering. But, in any case, ad-
mitting that my young wife from Aurillac had
been killed in an accident, the misfortune would
not be enough for me to be "the chosen one":
it was both too fortuitous and too common. My
fury thrust aside all obstacles; certain authors
who had been mocked and beaten had wallowed
in shame and darkness until their last gasp;
glory had crowned only their corpse. That's
what would happen to me! I would write con-
scientiously about Aurillac and its statues.

Incapable of hatred, I would aim only at recon-
ciling, at being useful. Yet, my first book would
create a scandal as soon as it came out; I would
become a public enemy, I would be insulted by
the local papers, shopkeepers would refuse to
serve me, fanatics would throw stones at my
windows, I would have to flee in order to escape
being lynched. Dumbfounded at first, I would
spend months in a state of daze, constantly repeating, "See here, it's all a misunderstanding!
Since everyone is good!" And indeed, it *was* only
a misunderstanding, but the Holy Ghost wouldn't
let it be cleared up. I would get over it; one day,
I would sit down at my table and write a new
book: about the sea or about the mountains. But
that one wouldn't find a publisher. Hounded,
disguised, perhaps banished, I would write others,
many others, I would translate Horace into
verse, I would expound modest and quite reasonable ideas on pedagogy. Nothing doing. My
notebooks piled up in a trunk, unpublished.

The story had two endings; I would choose
one or the other, depending on my mood. When
I was feeling low, I would see myself dying on
an iron cot, hated by everyone, desperate, in the
very hour when Glory was blowing its trumpet.
At other times, I would grant myself a bit of
happiness. At the age of fifty, in order to try out
a new pen, I would write my name on a manu-

script, which shortly thereafter would be mislaid.
Someone would find it, in an attic, in the gutter,
in a closet of the house which I had just left. He
would read it. Overwhelmed by it, he would
take it to Arthème Fayard, the famous publisher of Michel Zévaco. A triumph: ten thousand copies snapped up in two days. What
remorse in people's hearts! A hundred reporters
would go looking for me and not find me.
Recluse that I was, I remained unaware for a
long time of this sudden shift of opinion. Finally,
one day, I enter a café to come in out of the rain.
I notice a newspaper lying nearby and what do I
see? "Jean-Paul Sartre, the masked writer, the
bard of Aurillac, the poet of the sea." On page 3,
a six-column spread in capitals. I rejoice. No: I
am voluptuously forlorn. In any case, I return
home. With the help of my landlady, I tie up
the trunk containing the notebooks and ship it
to Fayard without giving my address. At this
point in my story, I would pause in order to
launch out into delicious schemes: if I sent the
package from the city in which I lived, the reporters would discover my retreat in no time. I
therefore took the trunk to Paris and had it delivered to the publisher by a forwarding agent.
Before taking the train, I went back to the scenes
of my childhood, the Rue le Goff, the Rue Soufflot, the Luxembourg. I was attracted by the
Café Balzar; I remembered that my grandfather

—who had since died—had sometimes taken me there in 1913. We would sit side by side on the bench, everyone would look at us knowingly, he would order a glass of beer and a small one for me, I felt I was loved. Now fifty years old and nostalgic, I pushed open the door of the café and asked for a small glass of beer. At the next table, some beautiful young women were talking animatedly; my name was mentioned. "Ah!" said one of them, "he may be old, he may be homely, but what does it matter! I'd give thirty years of my life to become his wife!" I looked at her with a proud, sad smile, she smiled back in surprise, I got up, I disappeared.

I spent a lot of time touching up that episode and a hundred others which I spare the reader. One can recognize, projected into a future world, my childhood itself, my situation, the concoctions of my sixth year, and the mopiness of my unappreciated paladins. I was still moping at the age of nine, and enjoying it immensely: by moping, the inexorable martyr that I was kept alive a misunderstanding which the Holy Ghost himself seemed to have tired of. Why not tell that ravishing admirer my name? Ah, I would say to myself, she comes too late. "But since she accepts me in any case?" "Well, it's because I'm too poor." "Too poor? What about the royalties?" This objection did not faze me: I had written to Fayard instructing him to distribute the money which was due me to the poor. Nevertheless, I had to finish the story. Well then, I would pass away in my little room, abandoned by all, but serene. Mission accomplished.

I am struck by one thing in that oft-repeated story: the day I see my name in the paper, something snaps, I'm finished; I sadly enjoy my fame, but I stop writing. The two dénouements come to the same thing: whether I die in order to be born to glory or whether glory comes first and kills me, the eagerness to write involves a refusal to live. At about that time, I was disturbed by an anecdote which I had read somewhere. It takes place in the last century. At a wayside station in Siberia, a writer is pacing up and down, waiting for the train. Not a single shack on the horizon, not a living soul. The writer's big, gloomy head weighs heavily on his shoulders. He is near-sighted, unmarried, coarse, and always in a temper. He is bored; he thinks about his prostate, about his debts. Suddenly, on the road running parallel to the tracks, appears a young countess in a brougham. She jumps out of the carriage and runs to the traveler, whom she has never seen but whom she claims to recognize from a daguerreotype that someone has shown her. She bows, takes the man's right hand, and kisses it. The story stopped there, and I don't know what it was supposed to mean. At the age of nine, I was amazed that that grumpy author found readers in the steppes and that such a lovely person came to remind him of the glory he had forgotten. It meant being born. More deeply: it meant dying. I could feel that; I wanted it to be so; a living commoner could not receive such testimony of admiration from such an aristocrat. The countess seemed to be saying to him: "If I've been able to go up to you and touch you, it's because there's no longer even any need to maintain superiority of rank. I don't care what you may think of my gesture. I no longer regard you as a man but as the symbol of your work." Killed by a kiss on the hand: a thousand miles from Saint Petersburg, fifty-five years from the day of his birth, a traveler caught fire; his glory consumed him and all that was left of him was the list of his works in flaming letters. I saw the countess return to her brougham and disappear and the steppes sink back into solitude. At twilight, the train rushed by the station without stopping in order to make up for lost time. A shiver of fear ran down my back. I remembered *Wind in the Trees* and said to myself: "The Countess was death." She would come; one day, on a deserted road, she would kiss my fingers.

Death was my vertigo because I had no desire to live. That is why it filled me with such terror.

By identifying it with glory, I made it my destination. I wanted to die. Horror sometimes froze
my impatience, but never for long. My sacred
joy would spring up again, I would await the
instant of lightning when I would burst into
flame and burn to the bone. Our deeper intentions are plans and evasions which are insepa-
rably linked. I can see that, despite the bluffing
and lying, the mad enterprise of writing in order
to be forgiven for my existence had a certain
reality. The proof is that I'm still writing fifty
years later. But if I go back to the origins, I
see there a flight forward, a simple-minded kind
of suicide. Yes, more than the epic, more than
martyrdom, it was death that I was seeking. For
a long time I had been afraid of ending as I had
begun, anywhere, in any which way, and I feared
that this vague decease would be only a reflection
of my vague birth. My vocation changed everything: the sword-strokes fly off, the writings remain; I discovered that in belles-lettres the Giver
can be transformed into his own Gift, that is,
into a pure object. Chance had made me a man,
generosity would make me a book. I could cast
my missive, my mind, in letters of bronze; I could
replace the rumblings of my life by irreplaceable
inscriptions, my flesh by a style, the faint spirals
of time by eternity, I could appear to the Holy
Ghost as a precipitate of language, could become an obsession to the species, could, in short,

be *other,* other than myself, other than the others, other than everything. I would start by giving myself an indestructible body and then I would hand myself over to the consumers. I would not write for the pleasure of writing, but in order to carve that glorious body in words. Viewed from the height of my tomb, my birth appeared to me as a necessary evil, as a quite provisional embodiment that prepared for my transfiguration: in order to be reborn, I had to write; in order to write, I needed a brain, eyes, arms. When the work was done, those organs would be automatically resorbed. Around 1955, a larva would burst open, twenty-five folio butterflies would emerge from it, flapping all their pages, and would go and alight on a shelf of the National Library. Those butterflies would be none other than I: I, twenty-five volumes, eighteen thousand pages of text, three hundred engravings, including a portrait of the author. My bones are made of leather and cardboard, my parchment-skinned flesh smells of glue and mushrooms, I sit in state through a hundred thirty pounds of paper, thoroughly at ease. I am reborn, I at last become a whole man, thinking, talking, singing, thundering, a man who asserts himself with the peremptory inertia of matter. Hands take me down, open me, spread me flat on the table, smooth me, and sometimes make me creak. I let them, and then suddenly I flash, I dazzle, I command attention from a distance, my powers shoot through time and space, they blast the wicked, protect the good. No one can forget or ignore me: I am a great fetish, tractable and terrible. My mind is in bits and pieces. All the better. Other minds take me over. People read *me,* I leap to the eye; they talk to *me.* I'm in everyone's mouth, a universal and individual language; I become a prospective curiosity in millions of gazes; to him who can love me, I step aside and disappear: I exist nowhere, at last I *am,* I'm everywhere. I'm a parasite on mankind, my blessings eat into it and force it to keep reviving my absence.

This hocus-pocus succeeded: I buried death in the shroud of glory. I now thought only of the latter, never of the former, without realizing that the two were one and the same. At the present time, when I am writing these lines, I know that I've had my day, within a few years more or less. I clearly imagine—and I'm not too gay about it —my forthcoming old age and senile decay, the decay of those I love. My death, never. I sometimes intimate to my close friends—some of whom are fifteen, twenty, thirty years younger than I—how sorry I'll be to outlive them. They laugh at me, and I laugh with them, but it's no use and won't be any use: at the age of nine, an operation took from me the means of feeling a certain pathos which is said to be peculiar to our condition. Ten years later, at the Ecole Normale, this pathos would suddenly seize some of my best friends; they would wake with a start, in a state of fear or anger; I snored like a log. One of them, after a serious illness, assured us that he had experienced the pangs of death, including the last gasp. Nizan was the most obsessed of all. At times, when fully awake, he would see himself as a corpse; he would stand up, his eyes swarming with worms, would grope for his pork-pie hat, and would disappear. The next day we would find him, drunk, with strangers. Sometimes, in a student's room, these victims would tell each other about their sleepless nights, their anticipated experience of nothingness. They understood each other without having to go into detail. I would listen to them; I liked them enough to wish eagerly that I could be like them, but to no avail. All I could grasp and appreciate were the dismal commonplaces: one lives, one dies, one never knows who's alive or who's dead; an hour before death, one is still alive. I had no doubt that there was a meaning in their talk that escaped me. I would remain silent, jealous, in exile. Finally they would turn to me, annoyed in advance: "What about you? Does all that leave you cold?" I would throw up my arms as a sign of impotence and humility. They would laugh angrily, dazzled by the blinding awareness that they were unable to communicate to me: "Don't you ever think to yourself when you close your eyes in bed that there are people who die in their sleep? Haven't you ever thought while brushing your teeth: this time it's *it,* this is my last day? Haven't you ever felt that you had to be quick quick quick, that time was short? Do you think you're immortal?" I would answer, partly in defiance, partly so as to fall in with them: "That's it, I think I'm immortal." Nothing was more false: I had taken precautions against accidental death, that was all; the Holy Ghost had commissioned me to do a long and exacting job, he had to leave me time enough to carry it out. I was an honorary corpse; it was my death that protected me against derailments, congestions, peritonitis: we had made a date; if I showed up too soon, it wouldn't be there yet. My friends could find fault with me all they liked for never thinking about it: they were unaware that I didn't stop living it for a single minute.

I now admit they were right: they had accepted our condition in its entirety, including the anxiety it involves; I had chosen to be reassured; and it was quite true, fundamentally, that I thought I was immortal. I had killed myself in advance because only the deceased enjoy immortality. Nizan and Maheu knew that they would be savagely attacked, that they would be

yanked from the world alive, full of blood.
Whereas I, I lied to myself: in order to deprive
death of its barbarity, I had made it my goal
and had made my life the only known means of
dying. I was going quietly to my end, having no
hopes or desires other than what was needed to
fill my books, certain that the last burst of my
heart would be inscribed on the last page of the
last volume of my works and that death would
be taking only a dead man. Nizan, at the age of
twenty, looked at women and cars, at all the good
things of life, with desperate haste: everything
had to be seen and taken right away. I too looked
at them, but with more zeal than lust: I was not
on earth to enjoy things but to draw up a bal-
ance-sheet. It was a little too easy. Out of
cowardice and with a good little boy's timidity, I
had backed away from the risks of a free and
open existence, an existence without a providential guarantee. I had convinced myself that
everything was written in advance, better still,
was a thing of the past.

Obviously that fraudulent operation spared me
the temptation of loving myself. Threatened with
annihilation, each of my friends barricaded himself in the present, discovered the irreplaceable
quality of his mortal life, and thought himself
touching, precious, and unique. Each of them
loved himself. I, the dead one, did not love myself;

I found myself very ordinary, more boring than the great Corneille, and my individuality as a subject had no other interest for me than to prepare for the moment that would change me into an object. Was I therefore more modest? No, but more crafty. I was charging my descendants to love me instead of doing so myself. For men and women still unborn, I would some day have charm, a certain indefinable quality, I would be the source of their happiness. I was even shrewder and more cunning: I secretly harked back to that life which I found tedious, of which I had been able to make only the instrument of my death; I did that in order to redeem it. I looked at it through future eyes and it appeared to me as a touching and wonderful story that I had lived for all mankind, a story that, thanks to me, nobody need relive and that had only to be related. I was in an actual state of frenzy: I chose as my future the past of a great immortal and I tried to live backwards. I became completely posthumous.

It was not entirely my fault. My grandfather had brought me up in a state of retrospective illusion. Moreover, he was not guilty either, and I am far from holding it against him: that mirage is born spontaneously of culture. When the witnesses have disappeared, a great man's death ceases forever to be a disaster; time turns it into

a trait of character. An old defunct is dead by nature; he is dead at the time of baptism, neither
more nor less than at the time of extreme unction; his life belongs to us; we enter it at either
end or in the middle; we go up and down the
course of it at will. The reason is that chronological order has exploded. Impossible to restore
it. The personage runs no further risks and no
longer even expects the tickling in his nose to
end in sneezing. His existence has the appearance
of an unfolding, but as soon as we try to restore
a bit of life to it, it relapses into simultaneity.
Though you may try to put yourself in his place,
to pretend to share his passions, his blunders, his
prejudices, to revive bygone acts of resistance or
a touch of impatience or apprehension, you will
be unable to keep from evaluating his behavior in
the light of results which were not foreseeable
and of information which he did not possess or
from giving particular weight to events whose
effects left their mark on him at a later time but
which he lived through casually. That's the
mirage: the future more real than the present.
This is not surprising: in a life which is over,
the end is regarded as the truth of the beginning.
The defunct remains mid-way between being
and value, between the raw fact and the recon-
struction. His history becomes a kind of circular
essence which is epitomized in each of his moments. In the drawing-rooms of Arras, a cold,

simpering young lawyer is carrying his head
under his arm because he is the late Robespierre;
blood is dripping from it but does not stain the
rug; not one of the guests notices it, whereas we
see nothing else; five years will go by before it
rolls into the basket, yet there it is, cut off, uttering gallant remarks despite its hanging jaw.
This error of perspective does not disturb us because we recognize it; we have the means of correcting it. But the clerks of the period concealed
it; they fed their idealism with it. When, they
insinuated, a great idea wishes to be born, it req-
uisitions, in a woman's belly, the great man who
will be the carrier of it. It chooses his condition
and his environment; it determines the exact pro-
portion between the intelligence and the obtuse-
ness of his associates, plans his education, subjects him to the necessary ordeals, and composes
for him, by successive retouches, an unstable character whose ups and downs it governs until the
object of all this care explodes by giving birth to
it. This was never stated outright, but everything
suggested that the sequence of causes screened
an inverse and secret order.

I used this mirage enthusiastically to complete
the guaranteeing of my destiny. I grabbed hold
of time, pushed it head over heels, and everything became clear. It began with a dark blue
little book which was bedizened with showy and

somewhat faded gilt ornamentation and the thick pages of which had a corpselike smell. It was entitled *The Childhood of Famous Men*. A label certified that my uncle Georges had received it in 1885 as second prize in arithmetic. I had come across it at the time of my whimsical journeys, had leafed through it, and then rejected it with annoyance. Those chosen young creatures bore no resemblance to child prodigies. The only thing they had in common with me was the dullness of their virtues, and I wondered why anyone spoke about them. Finally, the book disappeared; I had decided to punish it by hiding it. A year later, I turned the shelves upside down trying to find it. I had changed; the child prodigy had become a great man who was having trouble with his childhood. What a surprise: the book had changed too. The words were the same, but they spoke to me about myself. I had a feeling that that book was going to be the ruin of me, I hated it, I was afraid of it. Every day, before opening it, I would go and sit by the window; in case of danger, I would let the real light of day enter my eyes. People who deplore the influence of Fantômas or André Gide now make me laugh: does anyone think that children don't choose their poisons themselves? I swallowed mine with the anxious austerity of a drug-addict. Yet it seemed quite harmless. The book encouraged young readers: good conduct and filial piety lead to everything, even to becoming Rembrandt or Mozart. The author recounted, in the form of short narratives, the very ordinary occupations of no less ordinary but sensitive and pious boys who were called Johann Sebastian, Jean Jacques or Jean Baptiste and who gave joy to their families as I did to mine. But the poison was this: without ever mentioning the name of Bach, Rousseau, or Molière, the author made a point of constantly inserting allusions to their future greatness, of recalling casually, by means of a detail, their most famous works or deeds, of contriving his accounts so artfully that it was impossible to understand the most trivial incident without relating it to subsequent events. He introduced into the tumult of everyday life a great, fabulous silence which transfigured everything: the future. A certain Sanzio was dying to see the Pope; he was so eager that he was taken to the public square one day when the Pope was due to pass by. The youngster turned pale and stared. Finally, someone said to him: "I suppose you're satisfied, Raffaello. Did you at least take a good look at our Holy Father?" But the boy replied with a wild look: "What Holy Father? All I saw was colors!" Another day, little Miguel, who wanted to become a soldier, was sitting under a tree and enjoying a novel about chivalry when suddenly he was startled by a loud clash: an old lunatic of the neighborhood, a ruined squire, was caper-

ing on an old nag and thrusting his rusty lance
at a windmill. At dinner, Miguel related the incident with such sweet, funny faces that he made
everyone roar with laughter. But later, alone in
his room, he threw his novel on the floor, stamped
on it, and sobbed for a long time.

Those children lived in a state of error. They
thought they were acting and talking at random,
whereas the real purpose of their slightest remarks was to announce their Destiny. The author
and I smiled tenderly at each other over their
heads. I read the lives of those falsely mediocre
children as God had conceived them: starting at
the end. At first, I exulted: they were my
brothers; their glory would be mine. And then
everything turned upside down: I would find
myself on the other side of the page, *inside the
book*: Jean-Paul's childhood resembled that of
Jean-Jacques and of Johann-Sebastian, and
nothing happened to him that was not broadly
premonitory. But this time it was at my grand-
nephews that the author was winking. *I* was
being seen, from death to birth, by those future
children whom I did not imagine, and I was sending them messages which to me were undecipher-
able. I shuddered, paralyzed by my death, which
was the true meaning of all my gestures. Ousted
from myself, I tried to go back up the page in
the opposite direction and find myself on the

reader's side. I would raise my head, I would ask
the light for help. But *that too* was a message.
That sudden anxiety, that doubt, that movement
of the eyes and neck, how would they be inter-
preted in 2013 when there would be two keys
for opening me, the work and the decease? I
could not get out of the book. I had long since
finished reading it, but I remained a character in
it. I spied on myself: an hour before, I had
chatted with my mother; what had I augured? I
would remember some of my remarks, I would
repeat them aloud; that got me nowhere. The
sentences slipped by, impenetrable. To my own
ears, my voice had a foreign ring; a thieving
angel was pirating my thoughts in my very head,
and that angel was none other than a light-
haired little boy of the thirtieth century who was
sitting at a window and observing me through a
book. With loving horror, I felt his gaze pinning
me down in my millenary. I shammed for him; I
concocted double-edged remarks which I let fall
in public. Anne Marie would find me at my desk,
scribbling away. She would say: "It's so dark!
My little darling is ruining his eyes." It was an
opportunity to reply in all innocence: "I could
write even in the dark." She would laugh, would
call me her little silly, would put on the light; the
trick was done; we were both unaware that I had
just informed the year 3,000 of my future in-
firmity. Yes, toward the end of my life, more

blind than Beethoven was deaf, I would work gropingly on my last book. People would say, with disappointment: "But it's illegible!" There would even be talk of throwing it into the garbage. Finally, the Aurillac Municipal Library would ask for it out of pure piety. It would lie there for a hundred years, forgotten. And then, one day, out of love for me, young scholars would try to decipher it; their entire lifetime would not be enough to restore what would, of course, be my masterpiece. My mother had left the room, I was alone, I repeated to myself, slowly, above all without thinking about it: "In the dark!" There was a sharp crack: my great-grand-nephew, out there, had shut his book; he was dreaming about the childhood of his great-grand-uncle, and tears were rolling down his cheeks. "Nevertheless, it's true," he would sigh, "he wrote in the dark!"

I strutted past children still unborn who were the very image of me. I brought tears to my eyes by imagining those I would make them shed. I saw my death through their eyes; it had taken place, it was my truth: I became my own obituary.

After reading the preceding passage, a friend looked at me anxiously: "You had an even worse attack," he said, "than I imagined." Attack? I'm not quite sure. My delirium was manifestly labored. As I see it, the main question is that of sincerity. At the age of nine, I remained far short of it; then I went beyond it.

In the beginning, I was sound as an apple: a little faker who knew enough to stop in time. But I worked hard; even when it came to bluffing, I remained a plugger. I now regard my tricks and jugglings as spiritual exercises and my insincerity as the caricature of an utter sincerity that was constantly grazing me and always eluding me. I had not *chosen* my vocation; it had been imposed on me by others. Actually, nothing had happened: some words tossed off by an old woman and Charles' machiavellism. But that was enough for me to be convinced. The grown-ups, who were installed in my soul, pointed to my star; I didn't see it, but I saw their fingers pointing; I believed in the adults who claimed to believe in me. They had taught me the existence of the great dead—one of whom was still alive— Napoleon, Themistocles, Philip Augustus, Jean-Paul Sartre. I did not doubt the fact: to have doubted would have been to have doubts about the adults. As for the last-named, I would have liked simply to meet him face to face. I gaped and writhed in an effort to bring on the intuition that would have filled me with joy. I was a frigid woman whose convulsions crave and then try to replace the orgasm. Is she shamming or just a little too eager? In any case, I got nowhere, I was always before or after the impossible vision that would have revealed me to myself. At the end of my exercises, I would still be dubious, having gained nothing but a fine state of jangled nerves. Nothing could confirm or deny my mandate, which was based on the principle of authority, on the unquestionable goodness of grown-ups. Sealed and beyond reach, it remained inside me but belonged to me so little that I had never been able, even for an instant, to have doubts about it and could neither dissolve nor assimilate it.

Faith, even when profound, is never entire. One must constantly prop it up, or at least refrain from ruining it. I was consecrated, illustrious. I *had* my tomb in Père Lachaise Cemetery and perhaps in the Pantheon; an avenue was named after me in Paris, as were public squares in the provinces and in foreign countries. Yet, at the core of my optimism I had a sneaking feeling that I lacked substance. At Saint Anne's Psychiatric Clinic, a patient cried out in bed: "I'm a prince! Arrest the Grand Duke!" Someone went up to him and whispered in his ear: "Blow your nose!" and he blew his nose. He was asked: "What's your occupation?" He answered quietly: "Shoemaker," and started shouting again. I imagine that we're all like that man. In any case, at the beginning of my ninth year, I resembled him: I was a prince and a shoemaker.

Two years later, I would have been considered cured. The prince had disappeared, the shoemaker believed in nothing, I had even stopped writing. The "novel notebooks" had been thrown out, mislaid, or burned and had made way for grammar, arithmetic, and dictation notebooks. If someone had crept into my head, which was open to all the winds, he would have come upon a few busts, a stray multiplication table and the rule of three, thirty-two counties with the chief town of each but not the sub-prefecture, a rose called rosarosarosamrosaerosaerosa, some historical and literary monuments, a few polite maxims engraved on stiles, and sometimes, like a scarf of mist hovering over this sad garden, a sadistic reverie. Not a single female orphan. No sign of a gallant knight. The words hero, martyr, and saint were not inscribed anywhere, not repeated by any voice. The ex-Pardaillan received satisfactory health reports every term: child of average intelligence, very well behaved, not gifted for the exact sciences, imaginative but not excessively, sensitive; quite normal, despite a certain affectedness which, moreover, was on the wane. But I had gone completely mad. Two events, one public and the other private, had swept away the little reason that remained.

The first was a genuine surprise: in July 1914, there were still a few evil-doers; but suddenly, on August 2nd, virtue took over and reigned; all Frenchmen became good. My grandfather's enemies flung themselves into his arms, publishers enlisted, the common people prophesied; our friends collected the great, simple comments of their concierges, postmen, and plumbers and repeated them to us; everyone made a fuss, except my grandmother, who was definitely suspect. I was thrilled: France was putting on an act for me, I put on an act for France. Yet the war soon bored me; it upset my life so little that I probably would have forgotten about it, but I took a dislike to it when I realized it was ruining my reading matter. My favorite publications disappeared from the newsstands; Arnould Galopin, Jo Valle, and Jean de la Hire abandoned their familiar heroes, those teen-agers, my brothers, who went around the world in a biplane, in a sea-plane, and who fought two or three against a hundred; the pre-war colonialist novels were replaced by war novels full of cabin boys, young Alsatians and orphans, regimental mascots. I detested those newcomers. I regarded the little adventurers in the jungle as child prodigies because they massacred natives, who, after all, were adults: being a child prodigy myself, I recognized myself in them. But these soldier children were left out of everything. Individual heroism wavered: against the savages, it was maintained by superiority of arms; what was to be done against the German cannons? There had to be other cannons, gunners, an army. Amidst the brave poilus who stroked his head and protected him, the child prodigy relapsed into childhood; and I relapsed with him. From time to time, the author, out of pity, would ask me to carry a message; the Germans would capture me; I had a few proud pat answers with which to retort and then I would escape; I would get back to our lines; my mission was accomplished. I would be congratulated, of course, but without real enthusiasm, and I failed to see the dazzled gaze of the widows and orphans in the paternal eyes of the general. I had lost initiative: battles and the war would be won without me; adults regained their monopoly on heroism. Occasionally I would pick up the rifle of a dead soldier and fire a few shots, but neither Arnould Galopin nor Jean de la Hire ever allowed me to charge with a bayonet. As an apprentice hero, I waited impatiently to be old enough to join up. No—or rather it was the mascot who waited, it was the Alsatian orphan. I would withdraw from them, I would close the booklet. Writing would be a long, thankless labor, I knew it, I would be as patient as I had to be. But reading was a revel: I wanted

every possible kind of glory right away. And
what future was I being offered? A soldier?
Nothing doing! When the poilu was isolated, he
was as ineffectual as a child. He attacked with
the others, and it was the regiment that won the
battle. I didn't care to take part in community
victories. When Arnould Galopin wanted to
single out a soldier, he could find nothing better
than to send him to the rescue of a wounded
captain. This obscure devotion irritated me: the
slave saved the master. And besides, it was only
a piddling exploit: in wartime, courage is a run-
of-the-mill affair; any other soldier would have
done as much. It drove me wild. What I preferred in pre-war heroism was its solitude and
gratuitousness: I could leave the dull, everyday
virtues behind me and invent *my* kind of man all
by myself, out of generosity. *Around the World
in a Sea-plane, The Adventures of a Paris Ur-
chin, The Three Boy Scouts,* all those sacred
texts guided me on the road to death and resurrection. And now, all of a sudden, their authors
had betrayed me: they had put heroism within
reach of everyone; bravery and the gift of self
became everyday virtues; even worse, they were
reduced to the rank of the most elementary
duties. The change of setting went hand in hand
with this metamorphosis: the collective mists of
the Argonne had replaced the one big sun and
individualistic light of the Equator.

After a lay-off of a few months, I decided to
pick up my pen and write *my* kind of novel in
order to teach those gentlemen a good lesson. It
was in October 1914; we had not left Arcachon.
My mother bought me some notebooks, all alike;
on their purple covers was a drawing of Joan of
Arc wearing a helmet; a sign of the times. Protected by the Maid, I began the story of Perrin
the soldier: he kidnapped the Kaiser, tied him up
and brought him back to our lines; then, in the
presence of the assembled regiment, he challenged him to single combat, downed him, and,
with his knife at the Kaiser's throat, made him
sign an ignominious peace treaty and give Alsace-Lorraine back to us. At the end of a week,
my tale bored me stiff. I had borrowed the idea
of the duel from the cloak-and-dagger novels:
Stoerte-Becker, outlawed member of a distinguished family, entered a thieves' tavern; insulted by the leader of the band, a colossus, he
beat him to death with his bare hands, took his
place, and emerged as king of the bandits just in
time to embark his troops on a pirate ship. The
ceremony was governed by strict and immutable
laws: they required that the champion of Evil be
considered invincible, that the champion of Good
fight amidst hooting and jeering, and that his unexpected victory chill the spines of the scoffers.
But I, in my inexperience, had violated all the
rules and done the opposite of what I had meant

to do: however hefty the Kaiser might be, he
was no Hercules; one knew in advance that Perrin, who was a magnificent athlete, would make
short work of him. And, in addition, the public
was hostile to him, our poilus screamed their
hatred at him. By a turn-about that left me nonplussed, Wilhelm II, a criminal but alone,
covered with spit and insults, usurped before my
very eyes the royal friendlessness of my heroes.

But that wasn't the worst of it. Until then,
nothing had either confirmed or belied what
Louise called my "lucubrations": Africa was
vast, far away, and underpopulated; information
was lacking; nobody was in a position to prove
that my explorers weren't there, that they weren't
shooting Pygmies during the very hour that I was
relating their combat. I did not go so far as to take
myself for their chronicler, but I had heard so often
of the truth of works of fiction that I thought I was
speaking the truth through my stories, in a way
that still escaped me but that would be glaringly
evident to my future readers. In that ill-omened
month of October, I witnessed, helplessly, the
telescoping of fiction and reality: the conquered
Kaiser, who was a product of my pen, had given
the order to cease fire; therefore, in all good logic,
peace *had* to be restored that autumn; but it so
happened that the newspapers and the adults
kept repeating morning, noon and night that we

were settling into the war and that it was going to drag on. I felt mystified: I was an impostor, I was writing nonsense that no one would want to believe; in short, I discovered the imagination. For the first time in my life, I reread myself. My face got red. Was it *I* who had indulged in those childish fantasies? I was almost ready to give up literature. Finally, I took my notebook to the beach and buried it in the sand. The embarrassment blew over; I regained confidence; I was dedicated, there was no doubt about it; quite simply, belles-lettres had their secret, which they would some day reveal to me. Until then, my age required that I be extremely reserved. I stopped writing.

We returned to Paris. I abandoned Arnould Galopin and Jean de la Hire forever; I could not forgive those opportunists for having been right. I held aloof from the war, that epic of mediocrity. Embittered, I deserted the present and took refuge in the past. A few months before, at the end of 1913, I had discovered *Nick Carter, Buffalo Bill, Texas Jack,* and *Sitting Bull*: these publications disappeared at the beginning of hostilities; my grandfather claimed that the publisher was a German. Happily, most of the back numbers could be found in the second-hand bookstalls along the quays. I dragged my mother to the Seine; we made a thorough search

of the stalls, one by one, from the Orsay Station
to the Austerlitz Station; there were times when
we brought back as many as fifteen installments;
I soon had five hundred. I arranged them in even
piles; I never tired of counting them, of uttering
their mysterious titles aloud: *A Crime in a
Balloon, The Pact with the Devil, Baron Mou-
toushimi's Slaves, The Resurrection of Dazaar*.
I loved the fact that they were yellowed, stained,
and dog-eared, with a strange odor of dead
leaves; they *were* dead leaves, ruins, since the war
had stopped everything; I knew that the final
adventure of the man with the long hair would
remain unknown to me forever, that I would be
forever left in the dark about the last investiga-
tion of the king of the detectives; those lonely
heroes were, like me, victims of the world conflict, and I loved them all the more for it. Merely
to gaze at the colored pictures on the covers was
enough to plunge myself into an ecstasy of delight. Buffalo Bill galloped across the plain, at
times pursuing, at times fleeing the Indians. I
preferred the Nick Carter illustrations. One may
find them monotonous: in almost all of them, the
great detective knocks someone out or gets black-
jacked. But these brawls took place in the streets
of Manhattan, wastelands edged with brown
fences or frail cubical buildings, the color of
which was that of dried blood. This fascinated
me; I imagined a puritanical, blood-stained city

engulfed in space and barely concealing the savannah on which it was built. Crime and virtue were both outlawed there; the murderer and the righter of wrongs, both of whom were free and sovereign, fought it out at night with knives. In that city, as in Africa, beneath the same fiery sun, heroism again became a perpetual improvisation. My passion for New York stems from that.

I forgot both the war and my mandate. When I was asked: "What are you going to be when you grow up?", I would reply amiably and modestly that I would be a writer; but I had given up my dreams of glory and my spiritual exercises. For that reason, the war years were the happiest of my childhood. My mother and I were the same age and were always together. She called me her knight attendant, her little man. I told her everything. More than everything: my repressed writing emerged from my mouth in the form of prattle. I would describe what I saw, what Anne Marie saw as well as I, houses, trees, people. I would assume feelings for the pleasure of telling her about them; I became a transformer of energy: the world used me to become speech. It would begin with anonymous chatter in my head; someone would say: "I'm walking, I'm sitting, I'm drinking a glass of water, I'm eating a piece of candy." I would repeat aloud my endless commentary: "I'm walking, mamma, I'm drinking a glass of water, I'm sitting." I felt I had two voices, one of which—it hardly belonged to me and did not depend on my will—dictated what was said by the other; I decided that I was double. Those mild disturbances continued until the summer; they exhausted me; I grew annoyed with them and ended by being frightened. "It talks in my head," I said to my mother, who luckily was not alarmed.

This did not mar my happiness or our union. We had our myths, our oddities of language, and our ritual jokes. For almost a whole year, I ended at least one sentence in ten with the following words, which I uttered with ironic resignation: "But that doesn't matter." I would say: "There's a big white dog over there. He's not white, but that doesn't matter." We got into the habit of relating the trivial incidents of our life to each other, as they occurred, in an epic style; we would refer to ourselves in the third person. We would be waiting for a bus; it would go by without stopping; one of us would then cry out: "They stamped their feet and called down curses," and we would burst out laughing. In public, we had our little collusions; a wink would be enough. In a store, in a tea-shop, the salesgirl or waitress would seem funny to us; when we left, my mother would say: "I didn't look at you. I was afraid of laughing in her face," and I would feel proud of my power: there weren't many children who could make their mother laugh just by a look. We were shy and afraid together. One day, on the quays, I came upon twelve numbers of Buffalo Bill that I did not yet have. She was about to pay for them when a man approached. He was stout and pale, with anthracite eyes, a waxed moustache, a straw hat, and that slick look which the gay blades of the period liked to affect. He stared at my mother, but it was to me that he spoke: "They're spoiling you, kid, they're spoiling you!" he repeated breathlessly. At first I merely took offense; I resented such familiarity. But I noticed the maniacal look on his face, and Anne Marie and I were suddenly a single, frightened girl who stepped away. Taken aback, the gentleman went off. I have forgotten thousands of faces, but I still remember that blubbery mug. I knew nothing about things of the flesh, and I couldn't imagine what the man wanted of us, but the manifestation of desire is such that I seemed to understand, and, in a way, everything became clear to me. I had felt that desire through Anne Marie; through her I learned to scent the male, to fear him, to hate him. The incident tightened the bonds between us. I would trot along with a stern look, my hand in hers, and I felt sure I was protecting her. Is it the memory of those years?

Even now, I have a feeling of pleasure whenever I see a serious child talking gravely and tenderly to his child-mother. I like those sweet friendships that come into being far away from men and against them. I stare at those childish couples, and then I remember that I am a man and I look away.

The second event took place in October 1915. I was ten years and three months old. It was no longer possible to keep me sheltered from the world. Charles Schweitzer swallowed his grudge and registered me in the Lycée Henri IV as a day-pupil.

In the first composition, I was last. Young feudalist that I was, I regarded teaching as a personal bond. Mlle. Marie Louise had given me her knowledge out of love; I had received it out of bounty, for love of her. I was disconcerted by the *ex cathedra* courses which were addressed to one and all, by the democratic coldness of the law. Subjected to those constant comparisons, my fancied superiority vanished. There was always someone who answered more quickly or better than I. I was too loved to have doubts about myself. I wholeheartedly admired my classmates and did not envy them. My turn would come. At the age of fifty. In short, I was ruining myself without suffering. Seized with barren panic, I would zealously turn in extremely bad work. My grandfather had begun to frown. My mother hastily asked for an appointment with M. Ollivier, my official teacher. He received us in his small, bachelor apartment. My mother put on her melodious voice. Leaning against her armchair, I listened to her as I looked at the sun through the dusty windows. She tried hard to prove that I was better than my work showed: I had learned to read by myself, I wrote novels. When she had run out of arguments, she revealed that I was a ten-month child: better baked than the others, more glazed, crispier as a result of staying in the oven longer. M. Ollivier, who was more sensitive to her charms than to my merits, listened attentively. He was a tall, lean, bald man, with a large head, sunken eyes, waxy complexion, and a few red hairs under a long, hooked nose. He refused to give me private lessons, but promised to "follow up" on me. That was all I asked for. I would watch his eyes in class; he spoke only for me, I was sure of it. I thought he liked me; I liked him; a few kind words did the rest. I became, without effort, a rather good student. My grandfather grumbled when he read my report card at the end of the term, but he no longer thought of taking me out of the lycée. In the following grade, I stopped getting special treatment, but I had got used to democracy.

My schoolwork left me no time for writing.
My new acquaintances made me lose all desire
for it. I had playmates at last! I who had been
left out of things in the park was adopted the
very first day as if it were the most natural thing
in the world. I couldn't get over it. The fact is
that my friends seemed closer to me than the
young Pardaillans who had broken my heart;
they were day-pupils, mamma's boys, studious
youngsters. That didn't matter, I was delighted.
I had two lives. At home, I continued to play
at being a man. But among themselves children
hate childishness; they are honest-to-goodness
men. A man among men, I left school every day
in the company of the three Malaquins, Jean,
René and André, of Paul and Norbert Meyre,
Brun, and Max Bercot. We ran yelling around
the Place du Panthéon. It was a moment of
grave happiness. I dropped the family play-acting. Far from wanting to shine, I laughed in
chorus with the others, I repeated their catch-
words and phrases, I kept quiet, I obeyed, I imitated my neighbors' gestures, I had only one
desire: to be integrated. Keen, tough, and gay, I
felt I was made of steel, that I had been delivered
at last from the sin of existing. We played ball
between the Hotel of Great Men and the statue
of Jean Jacques Rousseau; I no longer envied
M. Simonnot. To whom would Meyre have
tossed the ball after making a feint at Grégoire if

I hadn't been present, *I, then and there?* How dull and dismal my dreams of glory seemed compared to these flashes of intuition that revealed to me my necessity.

As bad luck would have it, they went out faster than they lit up. Our games "overexcited" us, as our mothers said, and at times transformed our groups into a unanimous little crowd that swallowed me up. But we could never forget our parents for long; their invisible presence made us quickly relapse into the shared solitude of animal groups. Aimless, purposeless, without a hierarchy, our society wavered between total fusion and juxtaposition. Together, we lived in a state of truth, but we could not help feeling that we were being loaned to each other and that we each belonged to closely knit, powerful and primitive communities that devised fascinating myths, were nurtured on error, and imposed their arbitrary demands on us. Coddled and right-minded, sensitive, open to reason, frightened by disorder, hating violence and injustice, united and separated by the tacit conviction that the world had been created for our use and that our respective parents were the best in the world, we made a point of not hurting anyone and of being courteous even in our games. Jeering and insults were strictly taboo; if anyone lost his temper, the whole group would surround him, calm him down, make him apologize. It was his own mother who scolded him through the mouth of Jean Malaquin or Norbert Meyre. Moreover, those ladies all knew each other and treated each other cruelly. They told each other our remarks, our criticisms, each boy's comments on all the others; we, their sons, hid from each other what the grown-ups said. My mother once returned indignant from a visit to Mme. Malaquin, who had said to her point-blank: "André feels that Poulou puts on airs." It didn't bother me, that was how mothers talked among themselves. I didn't hold it against André and didn't say a word to him about the matter. In short, we respected the whole world, rich and poor, soldiers and civilians, young and old, men and animals. We despised only the day-boarders and the boys who lived at school. They must have been pretty guilty for their families to have abandoned them. Perhaps they had bad parents, but that didn't help matters: children had the parents they deserved. After four o'clock, when the free day-pupils went home, the lycée became a den of thieves.

Such cautious friendships were bound to be somewhat cool. When vacation came, we separated quite cheerfully. Yet I liked Bercot. Being the son of a widow, he was my brother. He was handsome, frail, and gentle, and I never tired of looking at his long, black hair, which was combed in Joan of Arc style, But, above all, we both had the proud distinction of having read everything, and we would go off by ourselves to a corner of the playground to discuss literature, that is, to reel off over and over, and always with pleasure, the names of the works we had held in our hands. One day, he looked at me with a wild expression and confided that he wanted to write. We were together again later, in the graduating class. He was still good-looking, but tubercular. He died at the age of eighteen.

All of us, even the sober-minded Bercot, admired Bénard, a plump little boy who was always cold and who looked like a baby chicken. The repute of his merits had even reached the ears of our mothers, who were slightly annoyed by it but who were continually holding him up to us as a model without succeeding in disgusting us with him. Our partiality can be seen from the fact that he was a day-boarder and that we liked him all the more for it. In the evening, beneath the family lamp, we would think about that missionary who stayed in the jungle to convert the cannibals of the dormitory, and we felt less afraid. It is only fair to say that the boarders themselves respected him. I no longer quite see the reason for this unanimous agreement. Bénard was gentle, amiable, and sensitive; in addition, he was at the head of the class in everything. And besides, his mamma stinted herself for him. Our mothers did not associate with that dressmaker, but they often spoke to us about her to make us realize the grandeur of mother love. We thought only of Bénard: he was the torch, the joy of that unfortunate woman; we saw only the grandeur of filial love; in short, everybody was moved to pity by those worthy poor. Yet that would not have been enough. The truth is that Bénard was only half alive. I never saw him without a big woolen muffler. He would smile at us gently but said little, and I remember that he was not allowed to join in our games. As for me, I revered him all the more because his frailty separated him from us. He had been put under glass; he would greet us and make signs to us from behind the pane, but we did not go near him; we cherished him from afar because he had, in his lifetime, the unobtrusiveness of symbols. Children are conformists: we were grateful to him for carrying perfection to the point of impersonality. When he chatted with us, the insignificance of his remarks delighted us. We never saw him angry or too gay. In class, he never raised his hand, but when he was called on, Truth spoke through his mouth, without hesitation and without zeal, just as Truth ought to speak. He amazed our gang of child prodigies because he was the best without being

prodigious. At that time, we were all more or
less fatherless orphans. The male parents were
dead or at the front; those who remained behind
lost status, were less manly, and wanted their
sons to forget about them. Mothers held sway,
and Bénard reflected the negative virtues of this
matriarchy.

At the end of the winter, he died. Children
and soldiers don't bother their heads about the
dead. Yet forty of us sobbed behind his coffin.
Our mothers stood by; the abyss was covered
over with flowers. The result was that we regarded his decease as a special prize for out-
standing achievement awarded before the end of
the term. And besides, Bénard had been so little
alive that he did not really die; he remained
among us, a diffuse and sacred presence. Our
good morals went up a notch: we had our dear
departed, we talked about him in low tones,
with a melancholy pleasure. Perhaps we would
be taken away prematurely, like him; we
imagined our mothers' tears, and we felt we were
precious. But have I been dreaming? I have a
blurred memory of something frightfully clear:
that widowed dressmaker had lost *everything*.
Did I really choke with horror at the thought of
it? Did I have an inkling of Evil, of the absence
of God, of an uninhabitable world? I think so: if

not, why would Bénard's image remain so painfully clear in my rejected, lost, forgotten childhood?

A few weeks later, our class was the witness
of a singular event: during the Latin period, the
door opened and Bénard entered the room, accompanied by the concierge. He nodded to M.
Durry, our teacher, and took a seat. We all
recognized his steel-rimmed glasses, muffler, and
slightly hooked nose, and also his general manner, which made one think of a chick trying to
keep warm. I thought God was giving him back
to us. M. Durry seemed to share our amazement;
he stopped the lesson, took a deep breath, and
asked: "Family name, given name, parents' occupation." Bénard replied that he was a day-
boarder and the son of an engineer and that his
name was Paul Yves Nizan. I was the most flab-
bergasted of all. During recreation, I made advances to him; he responded; we became friends.
There was one detail, however, that made me
feel I was dealing not with Bénard but with his
satanic likeness: Nizan was wall-eyed. It was too
late to take this into consideration. What I had
liked about that face was the embodiment of
Good; I ended by liking it for its own sake. I was
caught in a trap: my inclination for virtue had
led me to prize the Devil. In actual fact, the
pseudo-Bénard was not that bad; he was alive,

that was all; he had all the qualities of his double, but withered. In him, Bénard's reserve tended toward concealment; when he burned with violent and passive emotion, he didn't yell, but we saw him go white with rage and stammer. What we took for gentleness was only a momentary paralysis. It was not truth that was expressed by his mouth but a kind of cynical and idle objectivity which made us feel uneasy because we were not used to it, and though, of course, he adored his parents just as we adored ours, he was the only one who spoke of them ironically. In class, he shone less than Bénard; on the other hand, he had read a great deal and wanted to write. In short, he was a complete person, and nothing amazed me more than to see a person with Bénard's features. Obsessed by this resemblance, I never knew whether to praise him for offering the appearance of virtue or to blame him for having only the appearance of it, and I kept shifting back and forth from blind confidence to unreasoned distrust. It was not until much later, after a long separation, that we became real friends.

For two years, these events and encounters suspended my ruminations without eradicating their cause. In actual fact, nothing had changed depthwise. I had stopped thinking about the mandate that had been lodged within me, under seal, by the adults, but it subsisted. It took possession of my person. At the age of nine, I kept an eye on myself, even in my worst excesses. At the age of ten, I lost sight of myself. I ran with Brun, I chatted with Bercot, with Nizan. During this time, my false mission, left to itself, took on weight and finally toppled over into my darkness. I stopped seeing it; it shaped me; it exercised its power of attraction on everything, bending trees and walls, arching the sky above my head. I had taken myself for a prince; my madness lay in my being one. A character neurosis, says an analyst friend of mine. He's right: between the summer of 1914 and the autumn of 1916, my mandate became my character; my delirium left my head and flowed into my bones.

Nothing new happened to me. I found intact what I had acted, what I had prophesied. There was only one difference: without knowledge, without words, blindly, I *carried everything out*. Previously, I had depicted my life to myself by means of images: it was my death causing my birth, it was my birth driving me toward my death. As soon as I gave up *seeing* this reciprocity, I *became* it myself; I was strained to the breaking-point between those two extremes, being born and dying with each heartbeat. My future eternity became my concrete future: it made every instant trivial, it was at the core of

the deepest attention, it was an even deeper state
of abstraction, it was the emptiness of all pleni-
tude, the light unreality of reality; it killed from
a distance the taste of a caramel in my mouth,
the sorrows and pleasures in my heart; but it
redeemed the most trifling moment by virtue of
the mere fact that this moment came last and
brought me closer to it; it gave me the patience
to live; I never again wanted to skip twenty
years and skim twenty more; I never again
imagined the far-off days of my triumph; I
waited. Every minute I waited for the next one
because it brought the following one closer. I
lived serenely in a state of extreme urgency: I
was always ahead of myself, everything absorbed
me, nothing held me back. What a relief!
Formerly, my days had been so like each other
that I sometimes wondered whether I was not
condemned to experience the eternal recurrence
of the same one. They had not changed much;
they still had the bad habit of slipping away with
a shudder; but *I* had changed: time no longer
flowed back over my becalmed childhood; rather,
it was I, an arrow that had been shot by order,
who pierced time and went straight to the target.
In 1948, in Utrecht, Professor Van Lennep
showed me some tests in which slides are used. My
attention was riveted by a certain card: it showed
a horse galloping, a man walking, an eagle flying,
and a motor-boat shooting forward. You were

asked to tell which picture gave you the greatest
feeling of speed. I said: "It's the motor-boat."
Then I looked with curiosity at the drawing that
had asserted itself so brutally. The motor-boat
seemed to be taking off from the lake; in a moment, it would be soaring above those wavy
wastes. The reason for my choice occurred to
me immediately: at the age of ten, I had the impression that my prow was cleaving the present
and yanking me out of it; since then, I have been
running, I'm still running. For me, speed is
measured not so much by the distance covered
in a given time as by the power of uprooting.

One evening, more than twenty years ago,
Giacometti was hit by a car while crossing the
Place d'Italie. Though his leg was twisted, his
first feeling, in the state of lucid swoon into
which he had fallen, was a kind of joy: "Something has happened to me at last!" I know
his radicalism: he expected the worst. The life
which he so loved and which he would not have
changed for any other was knocked out of joint,
perhaps shattered, by the stupid violence of
chance: "So," he thought to himself, "I wasn't
meant to be a sculptor, nor even to live. I wasn't
meant for anything." What thrilled him was the
menacing order of causes that was suddenly un-
masked and the act of staring with the petrifying
gaze of a cataclysm at the lights of the city, at

human beings, at his own body lying flat in the mud: for a sculptor, the mineral world is never far away. I admire that will to welcome everything. If one likes surprises, one must like them to that degree, one must like even the rare flashes which reveal to devotees that the earth is not meant for them.

At the age of ten, I aspired to like nothing else. Every link of my life had to be unforeseen, had to smell of fresh paint. I consented in advance to mishaps and misadventures, and it's only fair to say that I put a good face on things. One evening, the electricity went off; something was out of order. I was called from another room. I moved forward with my arms out and banged my head against a folding-door so hard that I broke a tooth. The incident amused me, in spite of the pain; I laughed at it, just as Giacometti later laughed at his leg, but for diametrically opposite reasons. Since I had decided in advance that my story would have a happy ending, the unforeseen could only be a delusion, novelty could only be an appearance; the exigency of mankind had settled everything by causing me to be born. I saw in that broken tooth a sign, an obscure monition that I would understand later. In other words, I preserved the order of ends in all circumstances, at all costs; I watched my life through my death and saw only a closed memory

from which nothing could escape, into which
nothing entered. Can anyone imagine how secure
I felt? Chance events did not exist: I was involved
only with their providential counterfeits. Newspapers gave the impression that random forces
prowled the streets and struck down the small fry;
I, the pre-destined one, would never encounter
any. Perhaps I would lose an arm, a leg, both eyes.
But all that mattered was the way things happened; my misfortunes would be only tests,
means for writing a book. I learned to put up
with trouble and sickness; I regarded them as
the first fruits of my triumphal death, as rungs
on the ladder that was leading me to my glorious
end. That somewhat brutal solicitude did not
bother me, and I was eager to prove worthy of
it. I regarded the worst as a guarantee of something better: mistakes themselves would be useful—which amounted to saying that I didn't
make any. At the age of ten, I was sure of myself. Modest and insufferable, I saw my defeats
as conditions for my posthumous victory. Even
though I were blind or a legless cripple, even
though I were led astray by my errors, I would
win the war by dint of losing the battles. I saw
no difference between the ordeals reserved for
the elect and the failures for which I was responsible. This means that, fundamentally, my crimes
appeared to me as calamities and that I regarded
my misfortunes as mistakes. The fact is that I

could not catch a sickness, whether it was the measles or a head-cold, without declaring myself guilty: I had been lacking in vigilance, I had forgotten to put on my coat, my muffler. I always preferred to accuse myself rather than the universe, not out of simple good-heartedness, but in order to derive only from myself. This arrogance did not exclude humility. I was all the more ready to think I was fallible in that my lapses were necessarily the shortest path to Good. I managed to feel, in the fluctuations of my life, an irresistible attraction that constantly forced me, even despite myself, to make further progress.

All children know they are progressing. Moreover, they're not allowed to forget it: "Further progress to be made . . . making progress . . . serious and regular progress . . ." Adults related the History of France to us: after the first Republic, which was shaky, there was the second and then the third, which was the right one: never two without three. Bourgeois optimism was epitomized at the time by the program of the Radical Socialists: increasing abundance of goods, elimination of poverty by the growth of enlightenment and the number of small freeholds. We young gentlemen were given a simplified version of it, and we discovered to our satisfaction that our individual progress went hand in hand with that of the Nation. However, very few wanted to rise

aboye their fathers. Most of them were only
waiting to be adults. They would then stop growing and developing. It was the world around
them that would spontaneously become better
and more comfortable. Some of us awaited that
moment impatiently, others looked forward to
it anxiously or regretfully. As for myself, before
being dedicated I grew up in a state of indifference; I didn't give a damn about the toga
praetexta. My grandfather thought I was tiny,
and he was upset about it. "He'll be short, like the
Sartres," my grandmother would say, just to
annoy him. He would pretend not to hear, he
would stand in front of me and look me up and
down: "He's growing!" he would say, without
much conviction. I shared neither his anxieties
nor his hopes: weeds also grow, which was proof
that one could become tall and still be bad. My
problem, then, was to be good *in aeternum*.
Everything changed when my life began to speed
up: it was no longer enough to do well, I had
to do *better* every hour of the day. I now had
only one law: to climb. In order to bolster up
my pretensions and conceal their extravagance,
I resorted to the common experience: I tried to
see the first effects of my destiny in the wavering
progress of my childhood. That real but moderate
and very ordinary improvement gave me the il-
lusory feeling that I was moving onward and up-
ward. As a public child, I adopted in public the

myth of my class and generation: one makes use of acquired knowledge; one capitalizes experience; the present is enriched by the entire past. But in solitude I was far from satisfied with it. I could not grant that one received being from without, that it was preserved by inertia, and that the impulses of the mind were the effect of earlier impulses. Born of a future expectation, I leaped ahead, luminously, in my entirety; each and every moment repeated the ceremony of my birth; I wanted to see the workings of my heart as a crackling of sparks. So why should the past have enriched me? The past had not made me. On the contrary, it was I, rising from my ashes, who plucked my memory from nothingness by an act of creation which was always being repeated. Each time I was reborn better, and I made better use of the inert reserves of my soul for the simple reason that death, which was closer each time, lit me up more brightly with its dim light. I was often told that the past drives us forward, but I was convinced that I was being drawn by the future. I would have hated to feel quiet forces at work within me, the slow development of my natural aptitudes. I had stuffed my soul with the continuous progress of the bourgeois and had turned it into an internal combustion engine. I subordinated the past to the present and the present to the future; I transformed a quiet evolutionism into a revolutionary and discontinuous catastrophism. A few years ago, someone pointed out to me that the characters in my plays and novels make their decisions abruptly and in a state of crisis, that, for example, in *The Flies,* a moment is enough for Orestes to effect his conversion. Of course! Because I create them in my own image; not as I am, no doubt, but as I wanted to be.

I became a traitor and have remained one. Though I throw myself heart and soul into what I undertake, though I give myself up unreservedly to work, to anger, to friendship, I'll repudiate myself in a moment, I know I will, I want to, and I'm already betraying myself, in the heat of my passion, by the joyful presentiment of my future betrayal. On the whole, I fulfill my commitments like anyone else; I am steadfast in my affections and behavior; but I am unfaithful to my emotions. Monuments, paintings, landscapes, there was a time when the last one I saw was always the finest. I annoyed my friends by alluding cynically or simply lightly —so as to convince myself of my detachment— to a common memory that might have remained precious to them. Because I did not love myself sufficiently, I fled forward. The result is that I love myself still less; that inexorable progression constantly disqualifies me in my own eyes: yesterday I behaved badly since it was yesterday,

and I have a foreboding of the severity with
which I shall judge myself tomorrow. Above all,
no promiscuity: I keep my past at a respectful
distance. Adolescence, manhood, the year which
has just rolled by, these will always be the Old
Regime. The New is ushered in this very hour
but is never instituted: tomorrow, everything
goes by the board. I've crossed out my early
years in particular: when I began this book, it
took me a long time to decipher them beneath
the blots. When I was thirty, friends were surprised: "One would think you didn't have parents. Or a childhood." And I was silly enough
to feel flattered. Yet I like and respect the humble
and tenacious faithfulness of certain people—
particularly women—to their tastes, their desires,
their former plans, to bygone red-letter days;
I admire their will to remain the same amidst
change, to save their memory, to carry to the grave
a first doll, a milk tooth, a first love. I have known
men who, in later life, slept with an aging woman
solely because they had desired her in their youth.
Others harbored resentment against dead people
or would have come to blows rather than recognize a venial error committed twenty years earlier. As for me, I don't hold grudges and I
obligingly admit everything; I'm always ready
to criticize myself, provided I'm not forced to.
In 1936 and 1945, the individual who bears my
name was treated badly: does that concern me?

I hold him responsible for the insults he swallowed: the fool wasn't even able to command respect. An old friend meets me; a display of bitterness: he has been harboring a grievance for seventeen years; in a specific situation I treated him inconsiderately. I vaguely remember that I defended myself at the time by counter-attacking, that I taunted him with his touchiness, his persecution mania, in short, that I had my personal version of the incident. I am all the more eager to adopt his; I completely agree with him, I heap abuse on myself: I behaved conceitedly, I acted selfishly, I'm heartless; it's a joyful massacre; I revel in my lucidity; to recognize my misbehavior with such good grace is to prove to myself that I couldn't act that way now. Would anyone believe it? My fairness, my generous confession only irritate the plaintiff. He has seen through me, he knows that I'm using him. He has a grudge against *me,* me alive, present, past, the *same* person he has always known, and here am I leaving him an inert corpse for the pleasure of feeling like *a new-born babe.* I end by losing my temper with that maniac who's digging up old bones. Vice versa, if anyone reminds me of some incident in which, so I am told, I appeared to advantage, I pooh-pooh the memory; people think I'm being modest, but it's quite the opposite: I'm thinking that I would do better today and *so much* better tomorrow. Middle-aged writers don't like to be praised too earnestly for their early work; but I'm the one, I'm sure of it, who's pleased least of all by such compliments. My best book is the one I'm in the process of writing; right after it comes the last one that was published, but I'm secretly getting ready to be disgusted with it before long. If the critics should now think it's bad, they may wound me, but in six months I'll be coming round to their opinion. But on one condition: however poor and worthless they consider the book, I want them to rank it above all my previous work. I'm willing to let them run down my whole output, provided they maintain the chronological hierarchy, the only one that leaves me a chance to do better tomorrow, still better the day after, and to end with a masterpiece.

Naturally, I'm not taken in. I'm quite aware that we repeat ourselves. But this more recently acquired knowledge undermines my old certainties without quite destroying them. My life has a few supercilious witnesses who won't let me get away with anything; they often catch me falling into the same ruts. They tell me so, I believe them, and then, at the last moment, I feel pleased with myself: yesterday I was blind; today's progress lies in my realizing that I've stopped progressing. Sometimes it's I myself who am my witness for the prosecution. For example, it

occurs to me that two years earlier I wrote a
page that I might be able to use now. I look
for it and don't find it. So much the better: out
of laziness I was going to slip an old passage
into a new work; I write so much better today;
I'll write it over. When I have finished the work,
I happen by pure chance to come upon the lost
page. Amazement: except for a few commas,
I expressed the same idea in the same terms. I
hesitate, and then I throw the superseded docu-
ment into the waste basket. I keep the new version; there's something about it that's superior
to the old one. In short, I fix things up: though
undeceived, I fool myself in order to keep feeling,
despite the fact that old age is creeping up on
me, the youthful exhilaration of the mountain-
climber.

At the age of ten, I was not yet aware of my
quirks and repetitions, and I was untouched by
doubt. Jogging along, chattering, fascinated by
the spectacle of the street, I was constantly shed-
ding my skin, and I could hear the old skins fall
on their predecessors. When I walked up the Rue
Soufflot, I would feel at each stride, in the gleam-
ing wake of the shop windows, the movement of
my life, its law, and the noble mandate to be
unfaithful to everything. I took my whole self
along with me. My grandmother wants to match
her dinner set. I go to a china shop with her.

She points to a soup-tureen on the cover of which are flowers and a red apple. It's not quite what she wants; there are, of course, flowers on her plates too, but there are also insects climbing up stems. The shopkeeper starts warming up too. She knows what the customer wants, she had the article, but they stopped making it three years ago. This pattern is more recent, a very good buy, and besides, with or without insects flowers are always flowers, aren't they? My grandmother doesn't agree. She persists: wouldn't it be possible to take a look in the stockroom? Oh, in the stockroom, of course, but it will take time, and the shopkeeper is alone, her clerk just gave up her job. I am relegated to a corner and told not to touch anything. They forget about me. I am terrorized by the fragility of the things around me, by the dusty sparkling, by the death-mask of Pascal, by a chamber pot with a picture of the head of President Fallières. Despite appearances, I'm a false minor character. Some authors push "utility actors" into the foreground and show the hero fleetingly in three-quarter face. The reader is not fooled; he has leafed through the last chapter to see whether the novel has a happy ending; he knows that the pale young man leaning against the mantel has three hundred and fifty pages to go. Three hundred and fifty pages of love and adventure. I had at least five hundred. I was the hero of a long story that ended happily. I had stopped telling myself that story. What was the use? I felt like a fictional character, that was all. Time was disposing of the puzzled old ladies, the imitation-pottery flowers, and the whole shop; the black skirts were fading away; the voices were becoming wooly. I pitied my grandmother; she would certainly not reappear in the second part. As for me, I was the beginning, middle, and end gathered together in a tiny little boy already old, already dead, *here,* in the shadow, among piles of plates taller than he, and *outside,* far far away, in the great dismal sun of glory. I was the corpuscle at the beginning of its trajectory and the train of waves that flows back on it after crashing into the buffer. Boxed in, pulled together, touching my tomb with one hand and my cradle with the other, I felt brief and splendid, a flash of lightning that was blotted out by darkness.

Nevertheless, boredom clung to me. At times discreetly, at times disgustingly, I yielded to the most fatal temptation whenever I could no longer bear it: as a result of impatience, Orpheus lost Eurydice; as a result of impatience, I lost myself. Led astray by idleness, I would sometimes hark back to my madness when I should have ignored it, when I should have kept it under control and focused my attention on external objects. At such times, I wanted to *fulfill* myself on the spot, to

take in with a single glance the totality that
haunted me when I wasn't thinking about it. A
catastrophe! Progress, optimism, the joyful be-
trayals, and the secret finality, everything which
I myself had added to Mme. Picard's prediction
would collapse. The prediction remained, but
what could I do with it? By wanting to save all
my moments, that empty oracle forbade itself to
single out any in particular; the future would
suddenly dry up and all that remained of it was a
carcass; I would again be confronted with my
difficulty of being and would realize it had never
left me.

An undated memory: I am on a bench in the
Luxembourg; Anne Marie has asked me to sit
beside her and rest because I have been running
and am overheated. That is at least the order of
the causes. I am so bored that I arrogantly reverse it: I ran because I *had* to be overheated so
as to give my mother an occasion for calling me
over. Everything leads to the bench, everything
has to lead to it. What is its role? I don't know
and at first I don't care. Not a single one of the
impressions that graze me will be lost. There is
one goal: I shall know it, my nephews will know
it. I swing my short legs, which do not reach the
ground. I see a man going by with a package, or
a hunchbacked woman: I can use that. I repeat
to myself ecstatically: "It's of the highest impor-

tance that I remain seated." The boredom increases; I no longer refrain from peeping into myself: I am not asking for sensational revelations, but I would like to sense the meaning of that minute, to feel its urgency, to enjoy something of the obscure, vital foreknowledge which I attribute to de Musset, to Hugo. Naturally I see only a haze. The abstract postulation of my necessity and the raw intuition of my existence dwell side by side without conflicting or blending. All I want now is to run away, to regain the hot speed that whisked me along. In vain; the spell is broken. My foot's asleep, I twist and squirm. In the nick of time, Heaven charges me with a new mission; it's of the highest importance that I start running again. I jump to my feet, I'm off like a shot. At the end of the lane, I turn around: nothing has moved, nothing has happened. I hide my disappointment behind a screen of words: I assert that, around 1945, in a furnished room in Aurillac, this running will have untold consequences. I declare myself more than satisfied, I get excited. In order to force the Holy Ghost's hand, I let him in on the secret: I swear frantically that I'll deserve the chance he has given me. Everything is on edge, everything is keyed up, and I know it. My mother is already bearing down on me, here's the woolen jersey, the muffler, the overcoat. I let her wrap me up, I'm a package. I still have to deal with the Rue

Soufflot, the moustache of M. Trigon, the concierge, the creaks and groans of the hydraulic elevator. At last the woeful little pretender is back in the library; he wanders from chair to chair, turns the pages of books and thrusts them aside. I go to the window, I spot a fly under the curtain, I corner it in a muslin trap and move a murderous forefinger toward it. This moment is not in the program, it's something apart, timeless, incomparable, motionless, nothing will come of it this evening or later, Aurillac will never know about this cloudy eternity. Mankind is asleep. As for the illustrious writer—a regular saint, wouldn't hurt a fly—he happens to be out. Alone and without a future in a stagnant moment, a child is asking murder for strong sensations. Since I'm refused a man's destiny, I'll be the destiny of a fly. I don't rush matters, I'm letting it have time enough to become aware of the giant bending over it. I move my finger forward, the fly bursts, I'm foiled! Good God, I shouldn't have killed it! It was the only being in all creation that feared me; I no longer mean anything to anyone. I, the insecticide, take the victim's place and become an insect myself. I'm a fly, I've always been one. This time I've touched bottom. The only thing left for me to do is to pick up *The Adventures of Captain Corcoran* which is lying on the table, drop to the rug, and open at random a book I've read dozens of times. I'm so weary, so sad that I no longer feel my nerves and forget about myself as soon as I start reading. With his rifle under his arm and his tigress at his heels, Corcoran is driving game from cover; the jungle is hastily set up around them; far off, I have planted trees; monkeys are swinging from branch to branch. Suddenly Louison, the tigress, starts growling; Corcoran stops dead in his tracks: there's the enemy! It's this thrilling instant that my glory chooses for returning to its abode; at that moment, Mankind awakes with a start and calls me to the rescue and the Holy Ghost whispers its staggering words in my ear: "You would not seek me if you had not found me." This flattery will be lost: there's no one on hand to hear it, except the gallant Corcoran. The Illustrious Writer reappears on the scene as if that declaration were all he was waiting for; the blond head of a grand-nephew is bent over the story of my life; his eyes fill with tears; the future dawns; an infinite love envelops me; lights whirl about in my heart. I don't move; I don't even look at the great event. I quietly continue reading; the lights finally go out; I no longer feel anything except a rhythm, an irresistible impulse; I drive off, I have driven off, I keep going, the engine purrs. I feel the speed of my soul.

Such were my beginnings: I fled; external forces shaped my flight and made me. Religion,

which served as a model, could be discerned
through an outmoded conception of culture. Being infantile, it is closer to a child than anything
else. I was taught Sacred History, the Gospel,
and the catechism without being given the means
for believing. The result was a disorder which
became my particular order. There were twists
and turns, a considerable transfer; removed from
Catholicism, the sacred was deposited in belles-
lettres and the penman appeared, an *ersatz* of
the Christian that I was unable to be: his sole
concern was salvation; the only purpose of his
sojourn here below was that he merit posthumous
bliss by enduring ordeals in worthy fashion.
Decease was reduced to a rite of passage, and
earthly immortality was offered as a substitute
for eternal life. In order to assure myself that the
human race would remember me forever, it was
agreed in my head that the species would never
end. For me to expire in humanity's bosom was
to be born and become infinite, but if anyone put
forward, in my presence, the hypothesis that a
cataclysm might some day destroy the planet,
even in fifty thousand years, I would be panic-
stricken. Though I am now disillusioned, I cannot think about the cooling of the sun without
fear. I don't mind if my fellowmen forget about
me the day after I'm buried. As long as they're
alive, I'll haunt them, unnamed, imperceptible,
present in every one of them just as the billions

of dead who are unknown to me and whom I preserve from annihilation are present in me. But
if mankind disappears, it will kill its dead for
good.

The myth was quite simple, and I had no difficulty in digesting it. As I was both Protestant
and Catholic, my double religious affiliation kept
me from believing in the Saints, the Virgin, and
finally in God Himself as long as they were
called by their names. But a tremendous collective power had entered me. Lodged in my heart,
it lay in wait. It was the Faith of others. All that
was needed was to rename its customary object
and to modify it superficially. Faith recognized
the object beneath its disguises, which fooled me,
and then sprang at it, squeezing it in its claws.
I thought I was devoting myself to literature,
whereas I was actually taking Holy Orders. The
certainty of the humblest believer became, in my
case, the proud evidence of my predestination.
Predestined, why not? Isn't every Christian one
of the elect? I grew like a weed on the compost
of Catholicity; my roots sucked up its juices and
I changed them into sap. That was the origin of
the lucid blindness from which I suffered for
thirty years. One morning in 1917, in La Ro-
chelle, I was waiting for some schoolmates with
whom I was to go to the lycée. They were late.
After a while, not knowing what else to do to

occupy my mind, I decided to think of the Almighty. Immediately He tumbled into the blue and disappeared without giving any explanation. He doesn't exist, I said to myself with polite surprise, and I thought the matter was settled. In a way, it was, since never have I had the slightest temptation to bring Him back to life. But the Other One remained, the Invisible One, the Holy Ghost, the one who guaranteed my mandate and who ran my life with his great anonymous and sacred powers. I had all the more difficulty getting rid of him in that he had installed himself at the back of my head in the doctored notions which I used in my effort to understand, to situate, and to justify myself. For a long time, to write was to ask Death and my masked Religion to preserve my life from chance. I was of the Church. As a militant, I wanted to save myself by works; as a mystic, I attempted to reveal the silence of being by a thwarted rustling of words and, what was most important, I confused things with their names: that amounts to believing. I saw everything wrong. As long as the situation continued, I felt I was out of trouble. At the age of thirty, I executed the masterstroke of writing in *Nausea*—quite sincerely, believe me—about the bitter unjustified existence of my fellowmen and of exonerating my own. I *was* Roquentin; I used him to show, without complacency, the texture of my life. At the same time, I was *I,* the elect,

chronicler of Hell, a glass and steel photomic-
roscope peering at my own protoplasmic juices.
Later, I gaily demonstrated that man is impossible; I was impossible myself and differed from
the others only by the mandate to give expression
to that impossibility, which was thereby transfigured and became my most personal possibil-
ity, the object of my mission, the springboard of
my glory. I was a prisoner of that obvious contradiction, but I did not see it, I saw the world
through it. Fake to the marrow of my bones and
hoodwinked, I joyfully wrote about our unhappy
state. Dogmatic though I was, I doubted everything except that I was the elect of doubt. I built
with one hand what I destroyed with the other,
and I regarded anxiety as the guarantee of my
security; I was happy.

I have changed. I shall speak later on about
the acids that corroded the distorting transpar-
encies which enveloped me; I shall tell when and
how I served my apprenticeship to violence and
discovered my ugliness—which for a long time
was my negative principle, the quicklime in which
the wonderful child was dissolved; I shall also
explain the reason why I came to think systematically against myself, to the extent of measuring
the obvious truth of an idea by the displeasure it
caused me. The retrospective illusion has been
smashed to bits; martyrdom, salvation, and im-

mortality are falling to pieces; the edifice is going to rack and ruin; I collared the Holy Ghost in the cellar and threw him out; atheism is a cruel and long-range affair: I think I've carried it through. I see clearly, I've lost my illusions, I know what my real jobs are, I surely deserve a prize for good citizenship. For the last ten years or so I've been a man who's been waking up, cured of a long, bitter-sweet madness, and who can't get over the fact, a man who can't think of his old ways without laughing and who doesn't know what to do with himself. I've again become the traveler without a ticket that I was at the age of seven: the ticket-collector has entered my compartment; he looks at me, less severely than in the past; in fact, all he wants is to go away, to let me finish the trip in peace; he'll be satisfied with a valid excuse, any excuse. Unfortunately I can't think of any; and besides, I don't even feel like trying to find one. We remain there looking at each other, feeling uncomfortable, until the train gets to Dijon where I know very well that no one is waiting for me.

I've given up the office but not the frock: I still write. What else can I do?

Nulla dies sine linea.

It's a habit, and besides, it's my profession. For a long time, I took my pen for a sword; I now

know we're powerless. No matter. I write and
will keep writing books; they're needed; all the
same, they do serve some purpose. Culture doesn't
save anything or anyone, it doesn't justify. But
it's a product of man: he projects himself into it,
he recognizes himself in it; that critical mirror
alone offers him his image. Moreover, that old,
crumbling structure, my imposture, is also my
character: one gets rid of a neurosis, one doesn't
get cured of one's self. Though they are worn
out, blurred, humiliated, thrust aside, ignored,
all of the child's traits are still to be found in the
quinquagenarian. Most of the time they lie low,
they bide their time; at the first moment of in-
attention, they rise up and emerge, disguised; I
claim sincerely to be writing only for my time, but
my present notoriety annoys me; it's not glory,
since I'm alive, and yet that's enough to belie my
old dreams; could it be that I still harbor them
secretly? I have, I think, adapted them: since I've
lost the chance of dying unknown, I sometimes
flatter myself that I'm being misunderstood in my
lifetime. Griselda's not dead. Pardaillan still in-
habits me. So does Strogoff. I'm answerable only
to them, who are answerable only to God, and I
don't believe in God. So try to figure it out. As
for me, I can't, and I sometimes wonder whether
I'm not playing winner loses and not trying hard
to stamp out my one-time hopes so that everything will be restored to me a hundredfold. In

that case, I would be Philoctetes; that magnificent and stinking cripple gave everything away unconditionally, including his bow; but we can be sure that he's secretly waiting for his reward.

Let's drop that. Mamie would say:

"Gently, mortals, be discreet."

What I like about my madness is that it has protected me from the very beginning against the charms of the "élite": never have I thought that I was the happy possessor of a "talent"; my sole concern has been to save myself—nothing in my hands, nothing up my sleeve—by work and faith. As a result, my pure choice did not raise me above anyone. Without equipment, without tools, I set all of me to work in order to save all of me. If I relegate impossible Salvation to the proproom, what remains? A whole man, composed of all men and as good as all of them and no better than any.

About the Author

JEAN-PAUL SARTRE was born in Paris in 1905 and was graduated from the Ecole Normale Supérieur in 1929 with a doctorate in philosophy. While teaching in Paris during World War II, Sartre played a role in the French Resistance. His first play, *The Flies,* was produced in France, despite its message of defiance during the German occupation. In 1964 Sartre declined the Nobel Prize for Literature. He died in 1980.

No Exit and Three Other Plays, The Devil and the Good Lord and Two Other Plays, The Age of Reason, The Reprieve, Troubled Sleep, and *Search for a Method* are also available in Vintage Books.